Rediscover the gos[...] inspiring book, whi[...] ant stories ever told in surprising new ways. A blessing for anyone who wants to understand the gospels more fully and encounter Jesus more deeply. All that, plus some terrific illustrations too!

JAMES MARTIN, SJ,
author of **Learning to Pray**

Like a skilled weaver, Dan Daly, SJ, intertwines the gospel, Ignatian spirituality, and contemporary references into an intricate tapestry which rekindles our interest in stories that might have become overly familiar. Like Jesus, Daly knows the power of "once upon a time...." He hooks us with references to Nabal, the villainous son who does the right thing, an IHOP waitress who smokes like a fiend but knows life's too short for anger or criticism, an 1860s Denver newspaper editor, and eighteenth-century Italian violin makers. A motley, unlikely crew? Exactly! Fertile ground for lively stands on justice and hopes brimming over. This playful, creative, accessible portrait of Jesus might be just the nudge flagging followers or skeptical newcomers need to jump aboard his boat.

KATHY COFFEY, *author of*
More Hidden Women of the Gospels

This is not just a book of chapters but of meditations, taking us into the world of Jesus through alluring storytelling and engaging drawings and bringing the lessons of Jesus into our world, showing concretely how Jesus is speaking to me, here and now.

MARK E. THIBODEAUX, SJ, *author of*
Ignatian Discernment of Spirits in
Spiritual Direction and Pastoral Care

In *Jesus and the Barbecued Fish Breakfast*, Dan Daly, SJ, recasts beloved gospel stories, vividly setting scenes into which we may more easily enter and encounter Jesus. He draws parallels to our current-day realities, further enlivening the stories and bringing Jesus more deeply into our own lives. Thane Benson's delightful illustrations are jewels, magical iconic doorways into the stories in their own right. I highly recommend this book. It brings new meaning to "the joy of the gospel"!

PAULA SAPIENZA, *spiritual director at*
Sacred Heart Jesuit Retreat House

This book is a treasure. Fr. Dan Daly's deft hand as a storyteller leads the reader through a wide and accessible door to a community of scriptural friends. In the everydayness of their lives, we are invited to reflect on the whole of Christian experience, from the nature of inspiration to our own disquiet and longing for God. He has recast Ignatian contemplation in ways that would surely warm the heart of St. Ignatius Loyola.

STEPHANIE RUSSELL, EdD, *Vice President*
for Mission Integration, Association of Jesuit
Colleges and Universities

Jesus and the Barbecued Fish Breakfast

A Gospel Story Sampler Inspired by the Spiritual Exercises of Saint Ignatius

Dan Daly, SJ

ILLUSTRATED BY Thane Benson

TWENTY-THIRD PUBLICATIONS

twentythirdpublications.com

Imprimi Potest:
Very Reverend Ronald A. Mercier, SJ
Provincial, US Central and Southern Province of the Society of Jesus

Imprimatur:
Most Reverend Mark S. Rivituso
Auxiliary Bishop, Archdiocese of St. Louis

In accordance with CIC 827, permission to publish has been granted on January 30, 2020, by the Most Reverend Mark S. Rivituso, Auxiliary Bishop, Archdiocese of St. Louis. Permission to publish is an indication that nothing contrary to Church teaching is contained in this particular work. It does not imply any endorsement of the opinions expressed in the publication, or a general endorsement of any author; nor is any liability assumed by this permission.

TWENTY-THIRD PUBLICATIONS
One Montauk Avenue, Suite 200
New London, CT 06320
(860) 437-3012 or (800) 321-0411
www.twentythirdpublications.com

Artwork/Illustrations: Thane Benson

ISBN: 978-1-62785-637-9
Printed in the U.S.A.

 A division of Bayard, Inc.

CONTENTS

Acknowledgments from the author

I thank the members of my family, who have been a great blessing my entire life, and the Jesuits, a wonderfully inspiring and supportive company. I thank the parish and university faith communities of which I have been privileged to be a part and the many Scripture scholars and spiritual writers whose insights and explanations have brought the gospels to life.

I thank Mary Armijo, Kathleen Hughes, RSCJ, Randy Lumpp, and Mark Thibodeaux, SJ, whose feedback was invaluable, and the anonymous reviewers for the Society of Jesus and the Archdiocese of St. Louis for their thoughtful corrections and suggestions. Thanks, too, to Heidi Busse and Dan Connors, at Twenty-Third Publications, for their careful editing, and to Thane Benson, my collaborator on this project, whose illustrations always delight and inspire me.

Dan Daly, SJ

Acknowledgments from the illustrator

First and foremost, I want to thank my wife for her patience, encouragement, and enthusiasm throughout this project. I also want to thank my children for the inspiration they give me every day. And, finally, I want to thank my mother for being a steadfast example of faith in action throughout my life. One of my main motivations for wanting to work on this project was that I thought it would be something my mother would enjoy. I hope you like the book, Mom.

Thane Benson

Introduction

Everyone loves a good story. Families share stories about heroic grandparents who moved across the country to start a new life in the face of daunting obstacles. With great delight friends recount stories of shared misadventures during their time together in college. We get hooked on biographies of famous people whose early lives explain much about the history that follows and are equally fascinated by stories of ordinary people in extraordinary circumstances. And we love the movies, whether historical or make-believe. We crowd into theaters to enjoy big-budget productions that feature exceptional acting, amazing special effects, and, most especially, memorable stories.

The gospels are chock full of stories. Jesus was a master storyteller. He captivated the crowds with tales of wandering livestock, annoying neighbors, and devious employees. The stories were popular and memorable, passed down from one generation to the next and eventually preserved in the gospels of Matthew, Mark, Luke, and John. Of course, the gospel writers also included stories about Jesus and the people he encountered. They told stories about astrologers following a star, blind men regaining their sight, and Jesus sharing a meal with a collection of unsavory characters.

This book is a sampler of memorable gospel stories. I invite you to imagine the shaggy, forlorn sheep, the skeptical Samaritan woman pouring a cup of cool water for Jesus, and the angry money changer whose table was just overturned. I also invite you to join me in pondering what these stories might mean for us.

Stories are meant to be enjoyed. They also play a critical role in helping us understand our lives and our world and in connecting us with others. Family stories connect us with our histories and shape who we are. Engaged couples learn about each other and grow into an extended family through the tales they tell. We recount stories from our nation's history to remind us of who we are. Memorable stories from biographies or movies resonate with our own stories. They shed light on our experiences of courage, hope, or friendship. They tell us something about what it means to be human.

For those of us who are Christian, the gospels provide a special treasury of stories. These stories help us understand ourselves and the world from the perspective of faith. They help us know and grow closer to God and give direction to our lives. We believe that Jesus is God's great revelation to us and that we come to know Jesus through the stories about him. Moreover, the message Jesus wanted to share with us was very often in the form of stories. Jesus did not spell out many rules, really. He offered explanation and instruction on occasion but more often told us stories, stories to live by, stories that would shape our lives.

Included among those whose lives were forever changed by the gospel stories is St. Ignatius of Loyola, the founder of the Jesuits. In 1521, while still a knight in the service of a

Spanish duke, Ignatius was wounded in the leg while helping to defend the city of Pamplona from French attack. During his recovery he began reading a book on the life of Christ and another on the lives of the saints to help pass the time.

Ignatius still daydreamed about knighthood and der-ring-do, but little by little his imagination was filled with stories of Jesus and the saints. Ignatius noticed a difference in his imaginings. Tales of knighthood would deliver some brief enjoyment but would leave him feeling dry and dissatisfied. Stories of Jesus and the saints would pro-vide consolation and inspiration

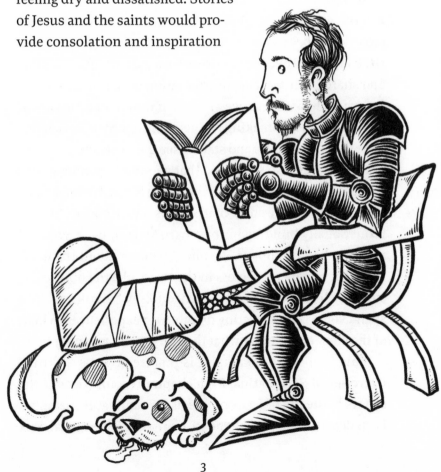

long after he finished reading them. Ignatius began to draw closer to God, to see his life in a different light, and to imagine new possibilities for the future.

Soon after he regained his health, Ignatius began composing a set of instructions that would help other people grow closer to God. Not surprisingly, gospel stories figured prominently in what would become his Spiritual Exercises. Ignatius invites us to contemplate gospel scenes, to put ourselves in the middle of the stories and let them play out. We hear what the characters say and watch what they do. We feel the hot sun, the wind, and the waves. We hear the possessed man bellow from the back of the synagogue and taste the fish cooked over an open fire. We are drawn into the story and share the hope, fear, or frustration of the characters. St. Ignatius knew that as we are drawn into the stories of the gospels, we begin making connections to other stories that have shaped our lives and start to see the world in a new way.

St. Ignatius also suggested that we simply ponder gospel stories to try to understand them a little better. We might consider a detail of the story that catches our attention, like the farmer busily building his new barn by lamplight while his family is having supper. We might wonder about the motivation of certain characters in the story, like the nine lepers cured by Jesus who never returned to say "thank you." We spend some time reflecting on our own experiences in light of the story and ponder what the story might mean for us.

This gospel story sampler is inspired by the Spiritual Exercises of St. Ignatius. Each chapter recounts one of the events in the life of Jesus or one of his captivating parables. I add details to help bring the stories to life. These details are not included in the gospels but are consistent with what we know about Jesus and the world in which he lived. I invite you to be drawn into the stories and let your imagination explore.

I connect the gospel narratives to other stories that have special meaning to me and resonate with my experiences. The stubborn refusal of people to acknowledge that Jesus healed a blind man reminds me of the equally stubborn response that Copernicus received. The adventures of the lost sheep remind me of the time I wandered aimlessly through the Bronx. I hope that you will be able to recognize connections with your own favorite stories. Making such connections enriches and sharpens the gospel accounts and brings those narratives into the constellation of stories that tell us who we are.

Finally, I suggest what the gospel accounts might mean for us. I propose how overflowing barns in ancient Palestine might be related to contemporary savings accounts and how people in our own day reveal as much faith and hope as the Jerusalem widow who happily contributed her two copper coins.

The stories are ordered chronologically for those who might like to follow the narrative from the beginning through to the end. But you can sample the stories in whatever way you like. Perhaps you will want to start with a few of your favorites before sampling a few that are a little less familiar.

We all love good stories, and the gospels are chock full of them. Stories enlighten us, change us, and connect us to others. I hope that this book provides an opportunity for you to discover and delight in the gospel stories again.

PART 1

Prologue

1
LUKE TOLD THE STORY WELL
Luke 1:1–4

Luke sat in the small, dusty courtyard outside his home at a makeshift table with pen in hand trying to collect his thoughts. He was composing a grand narrative of the life and teaching of Jesus for his patron, Theophilus. The family goat trotted by chewing on a recently completed parchment. Luke yelled at the goat, but it was too late; Luke would have to rewrite that chapter. Luke's eight-year-old son and eleven-year-old daughter rushed into the courtyard in the midst of a big argument that they wanted their father to settle. Before Luke could even begin to formulate a response, his wife stepped out from the house, wiping her hands on a towel, and corralled the two children. She explained that their father was trying to write a story. Such was life for our first-century Syrian author.

The author of the Gospel of Luke was a Greek-speaking Gentile living in Antioch, a large, bustling city in modern-day Turkey. He wrote the gospel sometime around AD 80. It is very likely that the author was Luke, one-time companion of Paul, who is briefly mentioned in the Acts of the Apostles. Although anonymous authors commonly attributed their work to a famous disciple like Peter, Paul, or John, no other author would attribute his work to Luke because Luke was not famous at all. Little-known Luke wrote the story and signed his name to it.

He might not have been famous, but he was talented. He was a good writer and employed a classical Greek style. Luke was smart, well-educated, and creative. He was familiar with both Jewish and Greek tradition and culture. In fact, Luke used so many big words that people think he might have been a physician. Luke stitched together stories from Mark's gospel and other sources in an engaging narrative that captures the essence of who Jesus is. Storytelling is an art, not merely a recitation of historical events. The way one frames or describes those events provides the underlying meaning and interpretation. Luke was very good at it.

The Gospel of Luke reminds us of the importance of storytelling. Stories provide meaning to the events of our lives. A college professor in Denver teaches a history course titled "The Stories from Wartime." He recognizes that the experience and meaning of war are not captured by facts and figures alone. On college retreats, student leaders share stories about their lives that interpret key events. For all of us, we grow in our faith and share faith with others through the stories we tell.

In writing the gospel story, Luke was inspired by the Holy Spirit. We do not know exactly how the Holy Spirit guided Luke, but it is unlikely that the author was drawn into a peaceful, mystical trance by which words simply flowed onto the parchment. The Holy Spirit does not work like that, at least not very often. The Holy Spirit usually works through human hearts, minds, and wills in subtle ways. We have to be open to that Spirit. And we must discern that Spirit, as St. Ignatius Loyola would say, because it is not always clear when we are being guided by the Spirit and when we are being guided by our own agendas.

St. Luke stayed connected with God through prayer on a regular basis. He worked at overcoming his fears, angers, and prejudices so that he would be free to write as God might have it. If our work is going to become God's work, we have to do the same things. We have to stay connected with God and prayerfully discern where the Holy Spirit might be leading us.

Of course, one of the most notable things about Luke's gospel is that it has survived to our own day. Plenty of people were writing stories about Jesus that were popular for a while but gradually dropped out of use. The Church eventually settled on four gospels to be included in the New Testament. The criteria were pretty simple. The gospels had to go back to the time of the apostles, to express well what Christians had come to believe, and to be widely read by the faithful. The Gospel of Luke was commonly used by small, local communities when they gathered for liturgy, first in Antioch and then in lots of other towns too. Luke's account told the story well and helped make Jesus present to the communities when they read it. Personally, I am happy that Luke's gospel made the cut. It has some terrific stories not found anywhere else: stories of Martha and Mary and Zacchaeus, parables of the good Samaritan and the prodigal son, the annunciation, the visit of the shepherds, and the appearance on the road to Emmaus.

This part of the history reminds us that a good story requires at least two people: someone to tell the story and someone to listen to it. The telling and the listening were important back in the first century and are important still. Theophilus and the people of ancient Antioch got to hear the story first. Now it is our turn. When we hear, enjoy, and ponder Luke's account and the other gospels, our faith grows and Jesus becomes present to us. May we continue to profit from listening to the words of this wise and talented man. May we too be open to God's Spirit in the work we are called to do.

Questions to ponder

■ *In writing his gospel account, how might Luke have known when he was being guided by his own agenda rather than by the Holy Spirit?*

■ *What story from your own life helps explain who you are today?*

■ *What is your favorite gospel story? Why do you like it?*

THE FIRST QUESTION AT THE END OF EACH CHAPTER PROVIDES AN OPPORTUNITY FOR FURTHER EXPLORATION OF THE STORY. THE NEXT TWO QUESTIONS SUGGEST POSSIBLE CONNECTIONS WITH YOUR OWN LIFE.

PART 2

First followers in Capernaum

2

GOD THE FATHER GAVE A TOAST

Matthew 3:13-17

Jesus sat on a bluff overlooking farmland south of Nazareth. The sun had just begun to rise, and the air was still cool. This particular spot was Jesus' favorite place to pray. He was going to miss this spot; he was going to miss Nazareth.

That morning, Jesus had decided that the time had come for him to bring words of encouragement to his disheartened countrymen. He would need to leave Nazareth so that he could spread the word far and wide. Jesus realized that God had high hopes and great affection for the people of Israel. Jesus needed to tell them about it.

After taking one last look at the farmland below, Jesus headed for home to break the news to his mother, Mary. Mary was mixing dough for flat bread when Jesus came inside and asked her to sit with him for a moment. As Jesus quietly explained his plans, Mary was not surprised. She knew that this day would come. Even so, her eyes filled with tears as she thought about how much she would miss him. When Jesus had finished explaining his plans Mary stood up and gave her son a hug.

Jesus spent the better part of the day announcing his plans to neighbors and other members of the family. They offered their best wishes and prayers and assured him that they would take good care of Mary. More than a few mentioned how proud Jesus' father, Joseph, would be. Jesus entrusted the woodworking business to his cousins and gave them the little bit of money he had saved. Early the next morning, Jesus grabbed his small traveling bag and skin of water and began his new life on the road.

His first stop was a wide expanse along the Jordan River where John the Baptist had set up shop. Jesus joined a crowd of people who listened to John's powerful words during the day and camped near the river's edge at night. Jesus spent several days simply listening to the prophet's instructions before finally wading into the water to be baptized. When Jesus reached the front of the line and knelt on the sandy riverbed, John paused for a moment, recognizing who Jesus was. After Jesus offered a word of encouragement, John plunged him into the clear, cool water. As Jesus stood up, water streaming from his hair, a voice came from the sky, saying, "This is my Son, my beloved, with whom I am well pleased." The crowd looked on in amazement.

We might say that God was offering a toast to Jesus, like a father would do today at the wedding of his son or daughter.

At a wedding reception the best man and the maid of honor each offer a toast to the happy couple. Sometimes the father of the bride or the father of the groom steps forward to offer a toast as well. It is a touching moment when Dad gets to say a few words about his daughter or son whom he loves very much and of whom he is very proud. The father provides a special insight into someone he knows very well but who is not so well known by all the guests in the room.

God took the opportunity to offer a toast to Jesus at his

baptism. It was short, sweet, and just right: "This is my Son, my beloved, with whom I am well pleased."

Each part of the toast has an Old Testament reference that tells us something about who Jesus is. "God's son" was a term used to describe King David, who had a special relationship with God and a very important role to play in leading the people of Israel. Sonship was an honor God also bestowed on David's descendants, including the Messiah who someday would save God's people. So, when God said of Jesus, "This is my Son," those gathered on the

banks of the Jordan River knew what it meant. Jesus was the long-awaited Messiah, the descendant of King David who would be a greater leader for the people of Israel.

Then God said more: "This is my Son, my beloved." God was pointing back to Isaac, the beloved son of Abraham. Abraham and his son, Isaac, after him, were the founders of the people of Israel. God wanted people to know that Jesus was part of the plan from the very beginning. Jesus is the fulfillment of promises made to Abraham, Isaac, and all those who would follow. And Jesus, like his ancestors, would be marked by special faithfulness to God's plans.

God concludes the toast with one more line. "This is my Son, my beloved, in whom I am well pleased." The last line refers to the faithful servant foretold by the prophet Isaiah, who would be rejected by his own people and endure great hardship and in whom God was well pleased.

Those who witnessed the wondrous epiphany that day understood the references to the Messiah, Isaac, and the suffering servant but were probably somewhat perplexed. Jesus was a poor peasant from Galilee. He did not have a palace, political influence, or an army at his disposal. How could he be a Messiah for his people? The Isaiah reference made things even more confusing. Isaiah prophesied that the faithful servant would be disdained. How could a Messiah be a Messiah if people refused to listen to his words?

We share the confusion of the crowd gathered on the banks of the Jordan River that day. God is trying to tell us something about Jesus, but we do not completely understand. We are not quite sure how Jesus saves us in our particular time and circumstances, so far removed from those of King David. We do not fully understand why Jesus was rejected and what the implications for our own lives are.

The first followers of Jesus grew gradually in their understanding, and so do we. We learn what it means for Jesus to be the Messiah and a faithful, suffering servant as we follow him through his public life, watch his actions, and listen to his words. We come to understand better Jesus' invitations to us as we spend more time with him.

One final thing about the toast God offered is worth noticing. The words were loaded with meaning, to tell everyone within earshot who Jesus is. At the same time, the words were loaded with affection. God did not simply say, "This is the Messiah, a descendant of King David," although that would have been sufficiently clear. God said, "This is my Son, whom I love." And God did not say, "This is my servant who will be rejected by his own people," but, "This is my Son, with whom I am well pleased." God spoke with great affection and pride for Jesus on that special day. No doubt Jesus was humbled by those words and filled with gratitude and joy. Those words would have stuck with him his whole life long.

Questions to ponder

- *In what ways did Jesus' life in Nazareth prepare him for his public ministry?*

- *Consider a major time of transition in your life. What were you thinking and feeling at the time?*

- *If God had said a few words about you at that time of transition, what might those words have been?*

3

DECISIONS FOR LIFE

Luke 4:1–13

Jesus headed east from the Jordan River into a strong wind, which slowed his progress but helped to dry his clothes, which were still damp from the river water. After a couple of hours he was in the middle of nowhere and decided to make camp. He needed some time to think and pray.

Jesus reflected on his life thus far, pondered the road ahead, and made some significant decisions. He made choices about how he would spend his time in the desert and, more important, how he would live the rest of his life.

Jesus fasted during his desert retreat so that he could focus his attention on matters more important than food. A couple of days after starting, he was hungry and considered getting some provisions. However, Jesus soon decided not to worry about what he was going to eat. Thoughts of food were a distraction; he wanted to focus his attention on prayer. More than that, Jesus chose not to worry about what he was going to eat for the rest of his life. Although he would certainly enjoy delicious meals and delightful wines in the future, Jesus was not going to worry about food. He was not going to plan his life around the next meal. On occasion he would run out of provisions or go to bed hungry. Life on the road was like that sometimes.

Jesus invites us not to worry about such things either,

about the food we are going to eat or the clothes we are
going to wear. In the grand scheme of things, food
and clothes do not make much difference. If we
get too preoccupied with department store
sales or our trip to the Bahamas, we will fail
to attend to other things that are much
more important.

Out in the desert, Jesus often took a
walk in the morning when the air was a

21

little cooler and signs of life were a little more evident. Jesus pondered the work he was about to undertake, the stories he might tell, and the places he might visit. During these reflections, the devil suggested how popular Jesus could become. If he crafted his message just right, Jesus could be a big hit not only in Judah and Galilee but also in Asia Minor, Greece, and maybe even Rome. Jesus recognized the temptation and decided that he would not sell his soul to the devil to be popular or influential. He wanted to listen to God's word and to follow God's directions, wherever that might lead. He would not compromise just to get a foot in the door or to be more successful.

Of course, Jesus did enjoy success. He was delighted when a big crowd would gather to listen to his words, but he did not tickle people's ears. He did not tell them nice things just to get them to come back. He never pandered to the powerful to win an endorsement.

On occasion Jesus would be invited to dine with Pharisees and teachers of the law. Jesus was pleased that he was making some inroads, that influential people were beginning to listen. Notwithstanding the nice invitations, Jesus continued to tell religious leaders that they were hypocrites who had little compassion and were leading the people astray. He pointed out their faults because it was the truth and they needed to hear it. The dinner invitations became far less frequent.

Jesus invites us not to sell our souls either. Popularity and influence are terrific. Perhaps we meet a few key people, make some connections, and suddenly start receiving invitations to elegant parties at beautiful homes in the heart of town. We drink Chilean wines, eat hors d'oeuvres, and chat with charming people who want to get to know us better. We enjoy the attention. Maybe we are a rising star in our organization. We receive a promotion, and the vice president takes us out to lunch. Suddenly, newer employees at the firm want to become our protégés; they seek us out for some advice. Influence and popularity are enjoyable.

But the elegant parties in the nice neighborhoods might come with some strings attached. We might need to temper our political views and buy a nicer car so that we fit in better. Elegant parties come with some expectations. Maintaining our rising-star status at the office is not easy either. We might have to work late during the week, come in on Saturdays, and generally cut down on the time we spend with our families. We might have to go along with top management, fire the troublemakers in the firm, and stop worrying about all the ethical implications of things.

Somewhere along the line we have to make a decision like Jesus did. Are we going to pursue the elegant parties, the promotions, and the protégés? Or are we going to stop worrying about those things and simply do what we need to do, come what may?

Out in the desert, Jesus made one more decision. He was sitting on a large outcropping of stone, watching the sky turn orange as the sun set, when he had this outrageous idea. The devil suggested that Jesus climb to the top of the tallest tower in the Temple and leap off so that God's angels would catch him. The devil reasoned that such a display would certainly convince people that Jesus was the Son of God. Jesus considered the possibility for a moment and then rejected it. Jesus would not seek the power to make people see or to change human hearts. He was a simple preacher from a dirt-poor family who grew up in the backwater town of Nazareth. He had never claimed any special power as God's Son and was not about to start now.

We do not claim any special power either. Sometimes we cannot get people to see what seems so perfectly clear to us. Sometimes we cannot get people to make even the smallest leap of faith. Sometimes we lack the wisdom, the power, or the charisma to counter forces in the world that are moving in a different direction. Like Jesus, we do what we can, accept our limitations, and leave the rest to God.

Jesus prayed for forty days in the desert and made some important decisions. He decided to listen to God's word and to not worry about food, popularity, and the power to change people's hearts. Jesus invites us to do the same.

Questions to ponder

- *If Jesus had wanted to do so, how could he have attracted more attention with his healing miracles?*

- *On a scale of importance from 1 to 10 (10 being extremely important) how would you rate your family, your job, your health, good food, and nice clothes?*

- *What is an example from your life when you did the right thing knowing that it was going to make you less popular?*

4
APPRENTICES SEEING THE WORLD WITH NEW EYES
John 1:35-39

Wonderful violins were crafted in the town of Cremora in northern Italy in the seventeenth and eighteenth centuries. Several families of luthiers had workshops where master artisans would oversee the fashioning of the instruments. Talented young people would serve as apprentices. They would join the master luthiers as they shopped at local mills, searching for perfect pieces of maple and spruce. They would watch the luthiers carve the inside of the instrument in just the right pattern. Eventually, the apprentices would be allowed to do some carving themselves, under the watchful eye of the masters, who would then tap the wood to test for the right sound. They would take finished violins in their hands so that they could feel the weight, the shape, and the balance. Apprentices would stay with the master for several years until they had learned all they could about their craft.

Andrew and Philip became the first apprentices of Jesus. For several weeks they had offered their assistance to John the Baptist on the banks of the Jordan River. The words of John inspired them, and they fully expected to serve as his disciples for many years. However, one morning, as light

began to fill the sky to the east, John invited Andrew and Philip to the edge of the bluff on which they were camped and pointed out a man walking alone on the road back to Galilee. "Behold the Lamb of God," John announced. "You should follow him now."

The two disciples looked back at John, the confusion written on their faces. "I will always be grateful for your faithful service," John assured them, "but your new teacher must now grow in prominence and I must step back." Andrew and Philip nodded, quickly said their farewells, and hurried along the road to catch up with Jesus.

Still fifty yards away, Philip shouted a greeting to Jesus. Jesus turned and smiled as he saw the two disciples kicking up a cloud of dust as they trotted along. "Master, where do you stay?" asked Andrew as they approached, a clear indication that they wanted to join his company, to see what he did, to be his apprentices.

"Come and see," Jesus welcomed them.

In a few years, Andrew and Philip would have important work to do. They both became leaders in the early Church. But, before that, they spent time with Jesus. They heard Jesus in the early morning quietly step away to find a place to pray. They joined Jesus for breakfast and helped him plan the day. They marveled as he peacefully stood in the midst of a great crowd and patiently attended to the needs of each one who approached. They listened to his stories again and again and relaxed with him around a campfire as dusk gave way to night. Andrew and Philip came to see the world through the eyes of Jesus, and when the time came for them to venture forth on their own, they were ready.

As we remember the story of Andrew and Philip, we reflect on our own apprenticeships. All of us were apprentices when we first joined our Christian faith community, and all of us are apprentices still. We learn from other members. We listen to what they say and watch what they do, both in church and out. We learn about praying for what we need, asking for forgiveness, and serving one another. We learn what it means to be a follower of Jesus.

We learn from one another, and we learn from God. Perhaps God takes the initiative and extends an unmistakable invitation. Or maybe we take the initiative, like Andrew and Philip. We approach Jesus and ask him, "Where do you live? How do you live?" Jesus responds with a big smile on his face, "Come and see."

Spending time with Jesus is a wonderful thing. Being his follower is like making a violin; it takes time to learn the craft. So we listen to him, watch what he does, and begin to see the world through his eyes. We invite Jesus to be part of the hustle and bustle of our busy days. We spend some quiet time with him too so that we can better hear what he has to say. We spend time with Jesus over a cup of coffee, talking about family, friends, or work. We spend time with Jesus while reading a gospel story, perhaps revisiting a familiar account and discovering something new. Of course, we spend time with Jesus every time we gather with others to pray. We remember the stories of our faith. We remember that Jesus is present with us in those gatherings.

Spending time with Jesus is important. Sure, there is a lot of work to do; God's plans will keep us busy. However, the only way that we will be ready to carry out those plans is if we have spent time with God, listening, learning, and seeing the world through God's eyes.

Questions to ponder

- *How might Andrew and Philip have been influenced by Jesus simply by having breakfast with him?*

- *Who has provided you with an inspiring example of the Christian life?*

- *Have you ever had the sense of Jesus being present with you during a busy moment of the day?*

5
QUIET DOWN!
Mark 1:21–26

The Capernaum synagogue was remarkably still. The customary rustling and murmuring were all but absent. Jesus had the full attention of the crowd. Unlike the scribes who seemingly directed their lesson to the scroll over which they were hunched, Jesus put the scroll aside and spoke directly to the assembly as one friend might talk to another.

Jesus was wrapping up his presentation when a disheveled man standing in the back bellowed in a clear voice filled with rage, "What is your purpose here, Jesus of Nazareth? Have you come to destroy us?" The man glared at Jesus, his head twitching from side to side. "I know who you are—the..."

"Quiet!" Jesus shouted as he stepped down from the platform and moved toward the man. "Come out of him!"

The man began convulsing violently and wheezed, gasping for air. Jesus put his hands on the man's shoulders as the shaking stopped and his breathing returned to normal.

Throughout the gospels we hear several accounts of Jesus driving out demons. A consistent pattern is evident. The unclean spirits usually like to talk, and, when they do, Jesus tells them to be quiet.

Unclean spirits speak to gain control of the situation. Speaking is power. The gospel stories describe the power that unclean spirits had over the people they possessed. The unclean spirits trapped their victims, controlling their actions and their words. Those possessed by demons did bizarre things. They hurt themselves and withdrew from family, friends, and God. Perhaps the most dramatic example is the Gerasene demoniac, who lived in a graveyard outside of town, screaming and bruising himself with stones. Unclean spirits had power over people. Jesus wanted to take that power away, so he told the unclean spirits to be quiet.

In our own day, we do not often see dramatic cases of demonic possession, but less dramatic examples can be found. Voices play inside people's heads all the time. Those voices are powerful; they can influence what people think, say, and do. The voices might not come from unclean spirits; they might originate with people's worries and doubts or spring from the world around them, but the voices are real, powerful, and ensnaring.

In his Spiritual Exercises, St. Ignatius Loyola devotes a chapter to the discernment of spirits. He speaks of a good spirit and an evil spirit. He says, "It is the characteristic of the evil spirit to harass with anxiety, to afflict with sadness, to raise obstacles backed by fallacious reasonings that disturb the soul" (SE §315). Whether we describe the source of these problems as "an evil spirit" or "destructive thinking patterns" does not make much difference, because the effect is the same. People experience sadness and anxiety as if unclean spirits were at work in their lives, speaking words to harass and trap them.

During trying times, the voices work overtime. When people have been laid off from their jobs and cannot find work, the voices fill them with sadness and discouragement. The voices tell them that they are worthless failures, which, of course, is a lie. As financial institutions fail and stock prices plunge, voices fill people with fear. People begin to worry about things over which they have very little control and to close themselves off from others. Difficult days prompt people to lose hope and to focus on the power of hatred, corruption, and greed.

To the voices that play in people's heads Jesus says, "Be quiet!" Jesus has his own words to speak to those facing unemployment, financial insecurity, or hopelessness. Jesus offers words of encouragement and hope. He reminds us that God loves us like parents love their children. He invites us to put our trust in God and not be overly anxious. "Do not worry about tomorrow," Jesus urged. "Tomorrow will take care of itself. Sufficient for a day is its own trouble." Jesus encourages us not to give up hope in the face of difficulties. "The Kingdom of God is like a mustard seed," he explained. "It starts out small but, in the end, will grow into something magnificent." God is watching over the whole world; there is reason for hope.

In the Capernaum synagogue Jesus encountered an unclean spirit that liked to talk. Jesus continues to confront voices playing inside people's heads today. Jesus says to those voices, "Be quiet." Jesus speaks words of love, encouragement, and hope instead.

Questions to ponder

- *Why might the disciples have had trouble casting out demons themselves?*

- *At what times in your life is the evil spirit most likely to harass you with anxiety?*

- *What lie does the evil spirit most like to tell you?*

6
A LOST SHEEP CHASING BUTTERFLIES
Luke 15:1–7

At the southern edge of the market in Tiberias, an enterprising vendor sold bowls of porridge and yogurt to those who had no families with whom to share a noontime meal. The patrons included prostitutes, tax collectors, and other unseemly characters who often gathered in the shade of a nearby mastic tree to enjoy a little food, wine, and conversation. Jesus, having just arrived in town, joined the group for lunch. A nosey Pharisee observed the gathering as he walked by and could not resist making a sarcastic comment, "Nice company you keep, Jesus."

"Perez, come join us," Jesus responded, "I was just about to tell a story."

After a little coaxing, Perez took a seat on the periphery of the group. Jesus began his story about a foolish sheep that wandered away from the flock and got terribly lost.

I can sympathize with the silly sheep. I have been lost a time or two myself. A few years ago I got lost in the Bronx, on foot, with luggage. An unfortunate predicament. I was trying to get to Fordham University so took the subway to the Fordham stop. (That seemed logical enough.) I came out of the subway station. No university was in sight. I walked toward a major cross street but saw nothing. I retraced my steps and headed toward a cluster of tall buildings; still nothing. A hill in the distance looked promising, so I started wandering in that direction. Soon I had no idea where I was.

The sheep that wandered away from the flock got lost quickly too. She headed off on her own toward a tree, since she liked to graze in the shade. She found no grass there so started following a butterfly. Then she got thirsty so started heading downhill. After a little while she looked around and wondered where the rest of the flock had gone. She decided to try to find them and started wandering in what seemed to be a promising direction, getting hungrier by the minute.

At times, we are like lost sheep. One minute, we are grazing with the rest of the flock, content and safe, with the shepherd nearby. The next minute, we are off on our own, hungry and confused and trying to figure out what to do next. Often, we have no great master plan; we do not intend to get lost. We start pursuing what seems to be a good idea at the time, one thing leads to another, and soon we are wandering around, completely off track.

Perhaps a woman has an argument with her brother-in-law. The disagreement is the type of thing that could get patched up with a phone call, but she never makes the call. Maybe she is tired, distracted, or stubborn. Whatever the reason, she never gets in touch with her brother-in-law, and he does not call her. The next time they see each other, the encounter is awkward. She makes a sarcastic comment, and he ignores it. The two start seeing each other less frequently and grow further and further apart. The woman has wandered off in the wrong direction and gotten lost.

Or maybe a middle-aged man starts growing dissatisfied with life. He is always reading about the rich and the famous and wishing his life were more like theirs. He encounters disappointments at work or at home and blows them out of proportion, failing to notice all the blessings that are part of his life too. The dissatisfaction gets in the way of hope, joy, and love. The middle-aged man has wandered off in the wrong direction and gotten lost.

Perhaps an account manager is not as honest as she once was. She used to be very conscientious about putting in a full day's work. Now she tells the boss that she is working at home when half the time she is really not. She goes out to lunch with a friend and charges it to a business expense. The lines get blurred, her standards shift, and she has gotten lost.

Part of the challenge of getting back to where we belong is realizing that we are lost. Several times as I was wandering around the Bronx with my roller bag, I was convinced I was on the right track. I was not. Similarly, the lost sheep did not realize that she was lost as she chased the butterfly around the pasture. In the same way, we can get so accustomed to broken relationships with family members that we fail to recognize when a problem exists. Padding our expense account can become second nature, and we forget that that is not the way things ought to be.

Even if we realize that we are lost, trying to fix things on our own does not always work and often makes things worse. I called a friend at Fordham on my cell phone but had to leave a voicemail message. While I was waiting for him to call back, I decided to keep searching for the elusive university, which, of course, meant I was getting further away by the minute. By the time the lost sheep started looking for the flock she was so far astray that she was never going to find it.

If we are experiencing dissatisfaction with life, we might try to solve things by going on a cruise. That might make us feel better for a while, but then the cruise ends, and we are more dissatisfied than ever, because we never got to the root of the problem. Or maybe we resolve to be more honest at work, trying to hold ourselves to higher standards. But our good intentions last about a week and then we start falling into the same old traps all over again.

Fortunately, we do not have to find our way back on our own. My friend at Fordham eventually called me back on my cell phone. He asked me where I was, and I told him the intersection. I was nowhere near Fordham. He told me to stay put and that he would come and get me. The sheep in the gospel story got rescued too. The shepherd realized that the sheep was missing and went to look for her. He found her in a dry riverbed, hot, tired, and dusty. So, he put the sheep on his shoulders and carried her back to the flock.

Like the shepherd in the story, Jesus wants to help us. He knows us well and realizes that we get lost from time to time. Jesus appreciates it when we can stay close to him but knows that we are not always able to do that. He worries about us; he wants to find us and bring us back. We do not have to do it all on our own; we just need to accept the help when it is offered. Jesus will set us on his shoulders and carry us back. From that vantage point we realize how far we have gone astray. We see how dry and deserted was the place to which we wandered and how green is the pasture to which we return.

Questions to ponder

- *Why is it easier for a shepherd to find a lost sheep than for the lost sheep to find the shepherd?*

- *Have you ever been geographically lost and made it worse by trying to fix things on your own?*

- *Have you ever been spiritually lost and made it worse by trying to fix things on your own?*

PART 3

An excursion to Jerusalem

7
AN UNEXPECTED CHAT
John 4:5–40

As I settled into my seat near the back of the large lecture hall at Harvard University, I felt decidedly out of place. Students were gathering for a course in adolescent psychology taught by a world-renowned feminist. I was neither a Harvard student nor a psychology major but a seminarian at the nearby Jesuit school of theology, cross-enrolled in a course that I hoped would be helpful in my future ministry. Of the two hundred students crowded into the hall, over 90 percent were women. I quietly pulled a spiral-bound notebook from my backpack, turned to the first page, brought pen to the ready, and hoped that no one would notice me.

Some of us might have the giant lecture hall experience when we attend to the words of Jesus. Whether we are listening to a gospel reading at church or reflecting on a Bible passage at home, we have the sense of sitting in the back row of an enormous lecture hall. The hall is filled with all sorts of people who have come to hear what Jesus has to say. We enjoy listening to Jesus and we learn much from him but stay in the back row, quiet and anonymous and feeling a little out of place.

Merab, a Samaritan woman in the little town of Sychar was content to live a quiet, anonymous life. One day, as she was running a few errands, she bumped into Jesus, who had stopped for a rest near the well at the edge of town. Jesus asked her for a drink. Merab was quite surprised that a holy man from Israel wanted to talk with her. Arching an eyebrow for extra emphasis, she asked the obvious question, "Sir, I am a woman and a Samaritan. Why do you want to have a cup of water with me?"

Jesus could not help but smile. He immediately liked the woman. Her gruff exterior failed to mask her sense of humor and refreshing candor. "If you knew who I was, you would ask me for living water," Jesus suggested.

"Where are you going to get this living water?" Merab quickly inquired. "You do not even have a bucket."

Jesus enjoyed talking with Merab. He knew that Jews were not supposed to talk with Samaritans and that men were not supposed to talk with women, but he did not care about that. Jesus wanted to get to know the Samaritan woman. He was not simply being nice out of sense of duty or obligation. His affection for her was genuine.

Somehow, Jesus knew that Merab's life was rather empty. She kept to herself and tried to be kind to others but never expected much out of life. If she had food to eat, clean water to drink, and a roof over her head she was satisfied. She had been married several times but never expected marriage to provide any more than some security and a little company. Jesus wanted her to know that there was more to life than that. Love, community, and service were possible. So too was a relationship with God, who watched over her and wanted to give her healing and hope. Jesus said, "If you drink the life-giving water I offer, you will never be thirsty again."

Merab understood the image and the invitation that Jesus was extending but was skeptical that God could work in the life of a poor, no-account sinner like her. She responded with sarcasm, "Please give me that water so that I don't have to keep coming out to this well!"

Jesus would not be deterred. He segued into a discussion of her five husbands to show Merab that he knew what her life was like. Jesus wanted to assure her that the messiness of her life did not stand in the way of the invitation he offered. Finally, Merab trusted enough to believe. "You are indeed a prophet," she said, bowing her head. "You honor us by your presence here. Please rest in the shade a while longer so that I can summon my neighbors and friends." Then she set down her bucket and hurried off to town to tell people of her remarkable encounter.

Jesus was hoping Merab would say something like that. He wanted to spread the good news to other people in the town of Sychar and needed some help. He needed an insider, someone who was a bit of a fighter, had a sense of humor, and was credible and candid. Jesus needed the woman at the well. After their conversation she became a missionary in her own hometown.

Where does that leave us? Maybe we are still sitting in the back of the big lecture hall listening to Jesus' words, confident that we remain unnoticed. Of course, we are not nearly as anonymous as we suspect. Jesus knows each one of us, even if we have never said a word to him, just like he knew the woman at the well. And Jesus likes us. When he reaches out to us, he is not just being nice. He has high hopes for us; he wants each one of us to have a great life, a life of love, community, and service. Perhaps Jesus has a special job that he needs us to do.

Most important, Jesus wants to be part of our lives; he wants to be that life-giving water that quenches our thirst, that heals us and gives us hope. Jesus is not asking for a dramatic change. He just wants a chance to talk once in a while, a little conversation between friends over something refreshing to drink.

Questions to ponder

- *By asking for a cup of water, how did Jesus facilitate his interchange with the Samaritan woman?*

- *Is it hard for you to imagine that Jesus is interested in your life? If so, why?*

- *In what ways do you proclaim the good news to neighbors and friends, either in your words or in your actions?*

8
NOTICING A WIDOW
IN A TATTERED SHAWL
Mark 12:41–44

Auction dinners are a very popular way to raise money for a good cause. Frequently the evening begins with a silent auction during which a person can bid on a big bucket of imported beer or dinner for four at Applebee's. The silent auction is for people who do not have much money but would like to donate a little something, especially if they can get some fajitas out of the deal. The silent auction is followed by a nice dinner and then an oral auction featuring the high-ticket items, like a vacation for two in Cabo San Lucas. The auctioneer starts the bidding: "1,500 dollars. Do I hear 1,500? 1,500? 1,500 dollar bid. Thank you, sir. Now 1,700. Now 1,700." And it keeps going. The auction is great entertainment. Everybody would like to go to Cabo, and $1,500 is real money. The winner gets a nice vacation and makes a generous gift that attracts some attention. Nobody cares much that I bid $25 for the bucket of beer.

The disciples had the same mind-set as they sat near the Temple treasury. They watched all the honorable and prosperous residents of Jerusalem make their contributions, failing to notice the widow in the tattered shawl deposit a couple of pennies in the collection box. But Jesus noticed her. He was not looking at the money. He was looking at the woman and saw something more than two copper coins.

He noticed that the widow was not worried a bit. She took the only money she had in the world and tossed it in the box. She trusted that God would take care of her. Jesus also noticed how much the woman loved the Temple, how she believed that God was present there. Jesus saw how much she loved God, how she just wanted to do something to show how grateful she was for all that God had done for her. Jesus noticed love, hope, and trust in God. He pointed out the widow to the disciples. He wanted them to notice her too.

Jesus was good at noticing people that others overlooked, like Zacchaeus the tax collector up in the tree. Others were trying to ignore him or missed him entirely, but Jesus saw him. He recognized that Zacchaeus was a man of integrity and holy desires. So he called Zacchaeus down and made plans for dinner.

Jesus noticed the woman with the hemorrhage who touched his cloak in the middle of a crowded street. The poor woman did not even want to be noticed, but Jesus found her and recognized her great faith.

Jesus saw something in Peter that others had missed. Jesus noticed his strength and bigheartedness and started calling him "Rocky" from the very first day. Jesus saw the humility and trust of the Roman centurion. Everyone else overlooked that. The Jewish people hated the Romans; seeing goodness in a Roman centurion was very difficult. Later, Jesus saw goodness in a sinful woman who came to wash his feet. He looked past her appearance and bad

reputation and noticed her great love instead. In a poor, blind beggar named Bartimaeus, Jesus saw hope shining through. Jesus noticed God's grace at work in all sorts of people. He told his disciples, "The harvest is already rich. You just need to go out and get it."

Jesus invited his disciples, and he invites us, to notice God's grace at work in the world. How can we hope for God's grace to come tomorrow unless we see it here today? He invites us to see grace at work in students, colleagues, and complete strangers. Grace is rarely extraordinary or dramatic. It is usually something simple, like the widow with the two coins.

If we walk across a college campus on a Monday morning, we can see first-year students heading to their classes. The students still have three and a half years of college left, but they have not given up. They still have hope that all their crazy work will make a difference. We can look at students and notice hope.

We can see goodness in people in the most unexpected places if we keep an eye out for it. One of the great gifts of working at a homeless shelter is the opportunity to see the goodness of the people who stay there. We can see people who have lived hard lives, filled with difficulties and disappointments, but who extend friendship or encouragement to others in the same predicament. We can look at people without a penny to their name and see love.

And if we want to see faith, we can just look around a church on Sunday morning. We see a wonderful collection of folks, young people and older couples, families, workers, and friends. Most of those who show up at church want to be there. Oh, there might have been a little arm-twisting, but most of us want to go to church because we believe that God is with us and because we want to be with God. We look around a church filled with people and we see faith.

If we keep our eyes open, we come to know that faith, hope, and love are possible because we can see them. The examples are not perfect, of course. There is some doubt mixed in with the faith, and fear combined with the hope, but the faith, hope, and love are real, just as they were for Zacchaeus, Peter, and the widow with the two copper coins.

Questions to ponder

- *Why did the poor widow want to contribute her two cents?*

- *Where have you seen faith, hope, or love in the life of someone you have encountered?*

- *Where might someone see faith, hope, or love in your life?*

9
REFUSING TO SEE
John 9:1–34

In the early 1500s there was a great astronomer by the name of Copernicus. Copernicus studied the sun and the moon. He looked through his telescope at night and studied the stars and the planets. He measured things and took lots of notes and did his calculations. Near the end of his life he published an amazing discovery: that the earth revolves around the sun, making the trip once every year. No one ever realized that before.

Copernicus told everyone about his discovery, but most people did not believe him. "Oh, Copernicus, you're crazy," they said. "The earth is not moving around; it's steady as a rock; the earth stays right where it is. The sun and the stars revolve around us. We are the center of the universe."

"No," Copernicus said, "that is only the way it seems. I have made all the measurements; I have done all the calculations. Here! See for yourself."

So the other astronomers checked all the measurements and calculations. The evidence was there, right in front of their noses, but they still could not see. They could not see because they did not want to see because Copernicus's discovery changed everything. It meant that the earth was not the center of the universe. This Copernican insight required a whole new way of looking at the world, and others were not ready to see the world that way yet.

Many people in Jerusalem were not ready to see when Jesus came to town and healed a blind man. The man was begging for alms just outside the Temple gate when Jesus and the disciples passed by. Jesus knelt in front of the man and asked if he wanted to be healed, and the blind man cautiously answered in the affirmative. Jesus spat on the ground and made a paste of clay that he smeared on the man's eyes. He instructed him to go to the Pool of Siloam and wash his face. The man did as instructed and came back able to see.

Unfortunately, several people with perfectly good eyesight refused to see what happened. First, they said, "Oh, no, this is not the blind man. This is just a fellow who looks like him."

But the blind man said, "No, I am the same guy who used to be blind."

Then the people said, "Most likely, he was never blind in the first place. He was probably just faking it."

So they asked his parents, who responded with incredulity, "He was not faking it! He was blind since the day he was born."

The crowd concluded, "Well, it must be some kind of witchcraft! God had nothing to do with it."

The blind man was astounded. "God had everything to do with it! Only God can heal like that. A person cannot cure blindness with witchcraft."

The people could offer no further explanations for the miraculous healing, so they simply responded, "Oh, you're just an old sinner; you do not know what you're talking about!"

Jesus cured the blind man right in front of their eyes, but

the people in the crowd refused to see. They did not want to see, because seeing what really happened would compel them to change their ways. In those days residents of Jerusalem thought that a person who was blind, sick, or poor was being punished by God for being a terrible sinner. Jesus tried to tell them that sickness is not a punishment. God is concerned about people who are blind or sick and wants to heal them. God hears the cry of the poor and wants to help them. By walking into town that day and healing the blind man, Jesus proved his point. God loved the blind man and wanted to help him.

The people in that town refused to see, because God's love for a blind man would demand a change from them. They knew that if God cares about people who are blind, sick, and poor, all of us better be concerned about them too. We should visit those who are sick and lend a hand to those who are blind. We had better make sure that the poor get enough to eat and have a warm place to sleep at night. If God cares, we should care too.

In addition, if the people in Jerusalem saw what really happened that day, they would have to admit that the blind, sick, and poor are not the biggest sinners in town and that the rich and the healthy are not the holiest saints. The world does not work that way. All of us are holy because we are created by God and because human life is holy. But all of us are sinners too; we all make mistakes and do things that are wrong. We all need God's forgiveness and help to get back on the right track. Residents of the city did not want to admit that.

In the early 1500s Copernicus made an amazing discovery, but many people refused to see, because acknowledging the insight would mean changing their ways of looking at things. In healing a blind man Jesus performed a wonderful miracle, but many people in Jerusalem refused to see it, because seeing would require a big change.

Jesus invites all of us to open our eyes, to see how much God loves the poor, the sick, and the blind and to recognize that we should care for those people too. He invites us to open our eyes to see that all of us are holy and all of us are sinners in need of God's help.

Questions to ponder

- *Do you think anyone other than the blind man came to greater faith in Jesus that day?*

- *What blind spot of yours might Jesus want to heal?*

- *What actions of Jesus challenge your preconceived notions of things?*

10
LET THE WEEDS GROW!
Matthew 13:24–30

Around the same time as Copernicus, the Inquisition was very busy trying to root out heretics who were considered a threat to the Church. Included on their list of suspects was St. Ignatius of Loyola, the future founder of the Jesuits. No surprise there, I suppose.

After his conversion but before he established the order, Ignatius was studying at the University of Alcalá in Spain. In his spare time he offered catechetical instruction and spiritual counseling to those who wanted it. Three things aroused concern: Ignatius was a layman, had no formal theological training, and was popular. Very suspicious! So one day the Inquisition paid a visit.

During their investigation they could find nothing wrong in what Ignatius said or did, so they left town. But the damage was already done. A cloud of suspicion hung over Ignatius and his companions. Some churches refused to give them Communion just in case they were heretics. A short time later, Ignatius was thrown in jail, accused of encouraging a rich woman and her daughter to leave Spain to become missionaries. Why that would merit jail time is not quite clear. In any case, he was released forty-two days later when the women returned and explained that they were just on a pilgrimage and had come up with the idea themselves.

Just to be on the safe side, the local authorities declared that Ignatius was prohibited from offering any further instruction or counsel. So Ignatius and his companions moved to a different town to continue their studies and their spiritual ministry. There was so much weeding out of heretics going on in Alcalá, Ignatius thought it best to try growing things in a different part of the garden.

Jesus proposed a parable to a group of listeners gathered just outside the Beautiful Gate. A man sowed good seed in his field, but his enemy snuck in one night and sowed weeds in the same field. When the crop grew, the weeds appeared as well. The farmhands volunteered to go through the field and pull up all the weeds. "No," the owner replied, "if you pull up the weeds you might uproot the wheat along with them. Let them grow together until harvest. We will get things sorted out then."

Jesus warns us against doing too much weeding. In fact, he recommends that we not do much weeding at all. He suggests that we let the weeds grow right along with the wheat. God will get it sorted out in the end.

One problem is that weeding is not an exact science. When we start pulling up weeds we inevitably uproot some good, healthy plants too. Telling the difference between the two is not always easy, especially if the plants are young or a little out of the ordinary. In the parable, the farm workers did not even recognize the weeds until the grain began to bear fruit. In a vegetable garden, if the peas and radishes are mixed in with the carrots, the young plants could easily be mistaken for weeds.

St. Ignatius and his companions were a little different from the other vegetables in the garden. Some Church leaders

were suspicious and did not want to take any chances. They tried to uproot Ignatius and the gang before things even started to grow. Ignatius managed to continue his work, but other good plants got destroyed during the Inquisition, and the garden was poorer for it. The parable is an invitation to let things grow in the garden, to appreciate the great variety, and to give the various plants a chance to bear fruit.

Once the plants have grown up it is easier to distinguish the weeds from the wheat. But even then, Jesus warns against doing too much weeding. Weeds and wheat grow so close together that disentangling them is difficult. They share the same soil, so if we disturb one we will likely disturb the other. Too much attention on getting rid of the weeds creates an environment of accusation, suspicion, and fear, making it tough for any plants to grow. That was certainly the case in Spain in the early 1500s. In the midst of all the accusations, restrictions, and prison time it was difficult for St. Ignatius to make much progress with his work. If he was not so stubborn he probably would have given up trying. An environment of encouragement and support would have been better then and is better now.

Such an environment does not mean that anything goes. Problems and failings within the community need to be addressed. On certain occasions a member of the community might need to be excluded for the safety and well-being of all. But exclusion should be an exception and a last resort. Weeding is not the order of the day. Rather, the community should be concerned about giving the good plants the water and fertilizer they need to thrive and worry about the weeds later.

A final problem with weeding in the world is that the distinction between weeds and wheat is never as clear-cut as it is in a garden. None of us is perfect. If we excluded from our community anyone with weed-like qualities, soon there would be no one left. We all share something in common with the weeds—and with the wheat too. There is goodness in all of us. Jesus certainly saw it. He saw goodness in tax collectors and in women caught in adultery, in Samaritans and in Roman soldiers. Jesus saw goodness in convicted criminals and in stubborn religious leaders. He recognized the hatred, greed, and fear that could take over people's hearts, but he kept extending a hand to try to lead them back. Jesus holds out hope that good fruit will come from even the prickliest of plants. He does not want us pulling up the weeds before he has given them every opportunity he can.

Questions to ponder

- *Why were the farmhands anxious to pull up the weeds in the farmer's field?*

- *In what way are you a little different from the other vegetables in God's garden?*

- *How does your local faith community provide space for a variety of vegetables to grow?*

11
LEGENDARY HOSPITALITY
Luke 10:38–42

Jesus sent word ahead to Bethany that he would be stopping for a short visit after Passover. When he arrived, he was surprised to see nearly one hundred people gathered to listen to him speak. The crowd was considerably larger than the one that assembled several months earlier, when Jesus first visited. Jesus knew that the increased enthusiasm was largely due to two sisters, Mary and Martha, friends and followers of his who had worked quietly but deliberately in spreading the word during the intervening months.

After speaking for more than an hour, Jesus made his way through the crowd to meet people and respond to their requests for healing and prayers. Mary stayed at Jesus' side while Martha left to prepare dinner. That was par for the course. Mary was wonderfully attentive to people but considerably less enthusiastic about household chores. In that regard, the two sisters made a good team. Whenever they hosted dinners, as they did frequently, Martha would do most of the meal preparation while Mary made sure that all the guests were made to feel right at home.

It is still true today that we need both Marthas and Marys to host a good event. I once helped host a dinner party when I was a member of a community of a dozen Jesuits in Detroit, a group comprised mostly of hard-working introverts. After the dinner plates were cleared, eleven of us were in the kitchen loading the dishwasher and putting away the food. The one Mary in the group had to come into the kitchen and herd the rest of us back into the dining room to entertain the guests.

When Jesus returned with Mary to the home of the two sisters, they found Martha in the courtyard, chopping vegetables to add to the pot of lentil stew simmering over the fire. Dough for flat bread was rising in a bowl near the clay oven that was not yet lit. Mary led Jesus to the second floor of the dwelling, offered him a pitcher and a basin so that he could wash his feet, and poured cups of cool water for them to drink. The table in the upper room was already set, complete with fresh flowers. Mary sat at the feet of Jesus and began asking about the lessons he had given earlier in the day. Before long, Martha appeared in the doorway, annoyed that her sister was so oblivious to all the work that still needed to be done and asked Jesus to instruct Mary to stop sitting around and start helping.

Jesus looked at Martha with a sympathetic smile. "Martha,

you are anxious about many things," he gently explained. "Only one thing really matters, and Mary is attending to that."

After a word of encouragement, Martha poured herself a cup of water and sat beside her sister as Jesus finished explaining the story he told earlier in the day. Then all three got up to finish the dinner preparations.

The meal was wonderful. The lentil stew was delicious, and the three friends talked long into the night about families, local politics, and Jesus' recent travels. For many years afterward, Mary and Martha remembered with fondness that wonderful evening with Jesus.

Jesus appreciated the hospitality of his two friends. When Jesus and the disciples were out on the road, they depended on the generosity of the people they met. They were always grateful when someone would offer them a good meal and a place to stay for the night. Perhaps Jesus met Martha and Mary on his first visit to Bethany, and the two sisters introduced themselves and invited him to dinner. It is consoling to know that good people scattered throughout Israel watched out for Jesus and offered him some hospitality whenever he passed through town.

Apparently, the hospitality of Martha and Mary was legendary. The gospel writers remembered it fifty years later. It is probably not too farfetched to think that one reason Martha and Mary were so well remembered was that their gracious hospitality continued after Jesus was gone. The two sisters appear in three stories in the gospels. Some of those who told the stories of Martha and Mary probably had visited their home and had enjoyed their cooking a time or two.

Jesus' visit with Martha and Mary is a story about friendship and hospitality. The episode also tells us something about discipleship. Martha's busy preparations are described as *diakonia* or "service." Jesus invited all his disciples to offer service. In addition, Luke reports that Mary sat at the feet of Jesus and listened to his words. Sitting at the feet of a teacher is the posture of a disciple. Luke is telling us that Martha and Mary were disciples of Jesus.

The fact that a first-century preacher in Palestine would have women as disciples was quite remarkable, but that clearly was the case with Jesus. Women gathered with the men to listen to Jesus speak. Women like Mary Magdalene traveled in his company. Martha and Mary sat at the feet of Jesus and listened to his words. If the two sisters did, in fact, continue to host meals in their home after Jesus had ascended to heaven, we can easily imagine that they also told stories about Jesus as they shared the meal in his memory, just like Jesus asked all his disciples to do.

In encouraging Martha not to worry about the dinner preparations, Jesus was making a point about hospitality. When we are hosting a party, we do not want to get so preoccupied with baking biscuits and preparing relish trays that we forget to enjoy the company of our guests. We do not want to lose sight of the bigger picture.

Jesus' instruction to Martha was also about discipleship. Clearly service is important. Jesus talked about it often. We are invited to live lives of service with our families, in the work we do nine to five, and in our efforts to help those in need. But Jesus reminded Martha and he reminds us not to get overworked and stressed out and forget to stay connected to him and the people in our lives.

Sometimes people with good jobs, who are making a valuable contribution, get trapped into trying to do too much, and what little free time they have gets taken up with home improvement projects and volunteer commitments. They do not have nearly enough time to relax with family, members of their community, or God. Jesus is inviting us to relax and sit with him for a while, learn what he might have to teach us, and tell him about our day. He invites us to enjoy his company as he enjoys ours.

We remember Martha and Mary, good friends of Jesus and the disciples, who were famous for their hospitality. They loved to share a good meal and a good conversation whenever Jesus and the gang came to town. Martha and Mary were also disciples of Jesus. They sat and listened to his words, and their lives were changed by his insights and example. After Jesus ascended into heaven, Martha and Mary continued to share stories about him, and the Church continued to grow. May we follow their example.

Questions to ponder

- *Why did Jesus make a special effort to invite women to be disciples?*

- *Are you more like Martha or Mary? In what ways?*

- *What role does hospitality play in your life?*

PART 4

Tough decisions on the road to Jericho

12
BUILDING BIGGER BARNS
Luke 12:16–21

The following spring, Jesus was back in Galilee with his disciples. Since Passover was only two weeks away, they began heading toward Jerusalem for the feast. Elisheba and Rezon, a middle-aged couple with no children, had traveled with Jesus for several months. Initially, they found his message very inspiring and were eager to support him in whatever way they could. Lately, however, Jesus had adopted a sharper tone, and his stories seemed to criticize honest, hard-working people like them. Rezon glanced at his wife and rolled his eyes as Jesus began his next story.

Amminadab owned a large grain field in the rolling hills of Judea. The farmer had two barns to store his harvest. Throughout the year he would take grain out of storage and bring it to the market to sell, providing a steady stream of income for his family. Amminadab also stowed away extra grain as an insurance policy in case the harvest the following year was disappointing.

Most of us make similar provisions. Instead of barns we have bank accounts and stock portfolios. We deposit our salary in a checking account so that we can draw on it to pay expenses throughout the year. We buy medical, property, and life insurance as a way of saving for a rainy day. We put money away for retirement and a college education fund so that we have enough for big bills down the road. We need checking accounts and retirement funds just like the farmer needed his barns.

One year, Amminadab was especially encouraged by his crop. The growing season had been ideal with just the right mixture of sunshine and rain and very few bugs. Heads of grain appeared like he never saw before. In addition, the grain field had been expanded the previous year. During the winter and early spring, Amminadab worked hard to clear a section of his property that had never been cultivated before. The seed that he had planted in that section was doing very well. The enlarged field and the perfect weather had combined for a bumper crop.

Sometimes we have a good year too and end up with more money than usual. Maybe we have a kindly aunt who remembers us in her will. Or maybe the boss gives us a big bonus. We are not quite sure what to do with all the money but take it anyway.

The large crop created a problem for Amminadab. His two barns would not be nearly big enough to hold the entire harvest, even if he cleared out all the remaining grain from the prior year. He could try to sell the surplus, but that was unlikely to work. Other farmers in the region would be bringing their grain to market too. The local townspeople could buy only so much grain. Amminadab realized that to take full advantage of the big harvest, he needed to build bigger barns. And that is exactly what he did.

We do not have the same problem when we have extra money. If we stashed our cash under a mattress we might run out of room, but we usually do not store our money there. We usually put our cash in the bank, and the bank always seems to have plenty of room for more. We do not run into the same predicament as the farmer with the extra grain.

Harvest was only four weeks away, so Amminadab had to work hard to erect his new barns in time. He hired a carpenter and two laborers and, together, they logged some long days to get the barns built. On many evenings the farmer was still digging post holes or sawing planks by lantern light while his family was eating dinner.

The barns were completed the day before harvest was to begin. That evening, as Amminadab looked out over his bumper crop and brand-new barns, he thought about how fortunate he was. He would have a sizeable stream of income for the next year and beyond. He could afford to hire a foreman to manage his property so that he could take more time off. He and his family now could enjoy fine wines and prime cuts of meat far more frequently than they had in the past. Amminadab was quite pleased. Just before he headed back inside, he heard God say, "Your life has now come to an end. Where will all your wealth go now?" And, with that, Amminadab died.

Building the bigger barns sounded like a good idea, but Jesus thought it was pretty foolish. It was foolish because the farmer did not need all that extra grain. Two regular-sized barns full of grain were enough to take care of his family for the coming year and to provide for a rainy day. He could have given away any extra. He did not even think of that option.

God had been so generous to Amminadab, he could have been generous with others. Many families in the area could use more grain than they could afford to buy. The farmer simply needed to find those families and give each of them a couple of extra bags of grain. But the farmer wanted it all for himself so that he could eat a little nicer food and drink a little nicer drink and swing in his hammock two hours every day. Anyone who focuses so much on himself and forgets about others is foolish.

It was foolish, too, to spend all that time clearing extra fields and building bigger barns. While he was working evenings and weekends, his family hardly ever got to see him. For what? So that he could have a nice steak every week? The farmer forgot that love, friendship, and the opportunity to serve are worth more than a big barn full of grain any day. And the farmer was foolish because he was always living for tomorrow and never appreciating today. If he had not been out in the dark building barns, he could have been inside enjoying a nice meal and a cup of wine in the company of family and friends. He could have appreciated what he had right now instead of wanting more in the future.

Followers of Jesus did not always find his stories easy to hear. Understandably, those who had some money in the bank wanted to hang on to it, and those without much money wanted to get a little more. In their view, Jesus was trying to deprive them of the little bit of happiness that money might provide. In actuality, Jesus wanted his followers to be truly happy and knew that money was not the answer.

Our struggles with money are much the same. Maybe it would help us if we had regular-sized bank accounts and retirement funds and the bank would call us to tell us when they were full. The bank representative would say, "Mr. Johnson, we just wanted to let you know that you have plenty of money right now. More than enough money for retirement, plenty of insurance for a rainy day. You can give all the rest of your money away." But they never do that, so we never know when to start giving it away. We get a $10,000 raise and, surprisingly, our annual expenses go up by the same amount. Or we put the money in the bank and start making plans for a bigger barn.

We are foolish like the farmer if we forget how generous God is with us and forget to be generous with others. We are foolish if we spend all our time worrying about a nicer home and a better vacation and fail to notice the people who need our help. We are foolish if we work evenings and weekends just so we can have a bigger barn and we miss the precious gift of family and friends. We are foolish if we are so busy planning for tomorrow that we forget to appreciate today. May God help all of us so that we are not foolish but grateful, generous, and wise.

Questions to ponder

- *The farmer with the bigger barns was probably not all bad. What might have been some of his admirable qualities?*

- *How do you know how much money you can afford to share with others?*

- *Was there ever a time in your life when you were so focused on tomorrow that you forgot to appreciate today?*

13

NO EARS TICKLED HERE

John 6:60, 66–69

The internet has some ludicrous advertisements for jobs. I saw one ad that announced, "Work at home and make $65 an hour!" When I clicked on the link to find out more, I was directed to a webpage that showed a woman who looked intelligent and professional. She was quoted: "I get paid about $25 for every link I post on Google and I get paid every week. I make around $15,500 a month right now."

Lest a visitor to the page think that special training was required, a reviewer's comment was prominently displayed: "You have to be able to use a computer at least somewhat. If you can use e-mail, etc. then you'll be fine." The job sounds ideal! Apparently, a person can earn $180,000 a year without any special skill or training.

Advertisements for exercise equipment are similar. One ad explains that the equipment is "designed so you can move through your workout fast." This speedy workout allows the user to burn calories, build muscle, and get a sculptured look. "Simple enough for beginners but powerful enough for serious training." What's not to like? You can buy the entire package for a mere $38 per month. The price sounds pretty good until you read the fine print about the contract term and the interest rate. According to my calculation, it would take a person about sixteen years to pay off the entire thing, which I suspect is about 15½ years longer that the average buyer remains interested in the workout regimen.

Advertisements try to tickle our ears, to tell us things we like to hear. We like to hear about great paying jobs that we can do in our pajamas. We like to hear that we can exercise how we want and for as long as we want and still get that sculptured look. These ads avoid telling us any hard truths, like the sixteen-year payment schedule, for example, lest we lose interest and search for a different website.

Jesus is not interested in tickling our ears, in telling us what we like to hear. Jesus tells us what we need to hear; he tells us the truth, even when it is not easy to understand or accept.

Jesus was up early to pray in Capernaum, so he noticed that several of those who had been traveling with him were heading back to their homes in towns and villages throughout Galilee. Some stopped to say goodbye and wish Jesus well. Others simply packed up and left, returning to the lives they had been living before they met Jesus. For many, his instructions and claims to be the bread of life were just too hard to hear. Perhaps they wanted to find someone who would tickle their ears.

At the same time, the apostles and a few other followers prepared to continue the journey with Jesus. They finished a quick breakfast, packed their bags, and checked signals about their next stop in Arbela. Jesus gave them a chance to change their minds. "Are you sure you want to stay with me?" he asked. "We might not be back in Galilee for a while."

Peter answered for the group, "Where else would we go? You have the words of life." The words of Jesus pointed them in the right direction, to the wonderful life that God had planned for them. The disciples did not always understand what Jesus was trying to tell them. They did not always find his instructions easy but found life in Jesus and in his words. There was nowhere else they would rather be.

Our experience is the same. We do not always understand what Jesus is trying to tell us. Sometimes his words are hard to hear, but we find a rich, satisfying, meaningful life in his company. We have come to put our hope in him. We stick with Jesus knowing that it will not always be easy.

Jesus says, "Blessed are the poor." Sometimes, those words are difficult to hear. They remind us that God has a special concern for the poor and that we are invited to share that concern and to reach out to those in need. That is not always easy to do. The words are difficult too because most of us are rich and further from God than we would like to admit. Nonetheless, we stick with Jesus because he speaks the truth. There are millions of poor people in the world, and we need to watch out for them, because we are all in this together. We stay close to Jesus because we are inspired by his vision and his hope; we seek the Kingdom of love and mercy he proclaims. We acknowledge that riches can sometimes get in the way of that. Sometimes we need the poor to show us the way.

Jesus says, "Love your enemies." Those words are sometimes hard to hear. They were difficult for followers in Jesus' day too. We do not like our enemies; we do not want to wish them well. But Jesus reminds us of the truth. Hatred and anger are not the answer; they only separate us from one another. Real life is found in love: love of family and friends and love of our enemies and opponents. If we show

Tough decisions on the road to Jericho

compassion toward only those who are lovable, we are not going to make much progress. God is love, and we will find life where we find love.

Jesus says that the last will be first and the first will be last. That sounds all mixed up to us. We like to keep everyone all lined up in a nice, neat order. We like to work hard and earn a place up front, but the truth is that none of us deserves a spot in the line at all. We could never begin to earn the blessings God continually showers on us. Fortunately, God opens the door wide; otherwise, we would never be able to sneak in.

Jesus is not interested in tickling our ears. He does not try to hide the hard truth from us, because the truth is too important, both the hard and the easy parts. Jesus does not promise things just because they sound good to us. Jesus has higher hopes for us than that. He tells us what we need to hear and continues to invite us to follow him. Where else would we go? Like Peter, we have come to believe that Jesus has the words of life.

Questions to ponder

- *Why did Jesus give the apostles a chance to change their minds and leave his company?*

- *What advertising claim sounds good but does not tell you the whole truth?*

- *What words of Jesus are the most difficult for you to hear?*

14

REMEMBERING TO BE GRATEFUL

Luke 17:12–19

The sun was already high in the sky as Jesus and his disciples neared a village on the edge of Samaria. A disheveled quintet with tattered clothes and gaping sores approached the road-way from an encampment in a stand of trees to the west. One of them announced, "Unclean," in case there was any doubt that they suffered from leprosy.

Soon five more lepers silently approached from the hills to the east. Although Jesus was traveling with a large group, the welcome party focused their attention solely on him. They all seemed to know who he was. With bended knees and bowed heads, they asked Jesus to have pity and heal them.

Jesus spoke a few words of encouragement to the sad assembly and then instructed them to present themselves to the priests in town. Members of the group looked at Jesus and one another with sadness and confusion, disappointed that Jesus was sending them away without healing them. Slowly they stood up and processed toward town to find the priest who lived there. On their way all ten were healed. Sadly, nine of those who had been afflicted with leprosy never returned to Jesus to acknowledge the great gift that they had been given.

Feivel stopped for a drink of water at a cistern on the edge of town. It was then that he noticed that the skin on his arms and legs was beginning to heal. He concluded that the ailment that had afflicted him for the past several months had finally passed. "It was not leprosy after all," he thought to himself, "but just a serious rash." Happy that the problem was behind him, Feivel hurried home to rejoin his family.

Bilhah sat for a moment to adjust a bandage on her lower leg. She had been applying medicinal ointments to her sores, hoping that the home remedies would improve her health. As she removed a bandage from her leg, she saw that a large sore had stopped bleeding and had begun to heal. Pleased with the success of her medical regimen, she returned to her tent to change the bandages and apply more ointment.

A small contingent of the original group located the priest at his home near the center of town. After some initial reluctance, he came out to investigate whether any healing had taken place. With growing amazement, he inspected the arms, legs, and faces of the visitors. At last, he declared, "You are all clean! Every one of you! May God be praised!"

Dinah and Gemariah were happy to hear that their leprosy was gone but did not take the time to appreciate it. They were now concerned about other things. Dinah wanted to see her family in Capernaum. She needed to buy a good pair of sandals and a traveling bag and try to find a group that was heading that way. Gemariah hardly had any money and was anxious to have a decent meal. So as soon as he was cured, he started looking around for work, hoping that a new employer might give him a little advance on his pay.

And so it went with nine of the ten lepers. None of them

took the time to appreciate what had happened to them and to thank Jesus who made it possible.

Sometimes we can be like those nine people with leprosy. Our uncle is going in for heart surgery, and it looks pretty serious. So we pray that God give him healing and strength. Then our uncle comes through the surgery with flying colors, and we think, "I guess it was not so serious after all."

We pray to God for some reconciliation with an old friend. Our friend gives us a phone call, and we have a good, long conversation. After the phone call concludes, we say to God, "Never mind. My friend and I worked things out on our own."

Part of the problem is that we can explain almost everything without reference to God, and we fail to recognize God at work in all those explanations. Maybe we figure God does not answer prayers because we do not always receive the answers we want. The gospel stories remind us that God loves us and hears our prayers and that God gives us gifts all the time, even when we have not asked for them. The story of the ten lepers invites us to notice and be grateful.

Sometimes we are like Dinah and Gemariah. No sooner is a prayer answered with a gift from God than we set our heart on something else. We finally land a job after three months of looking for work, and we immediately start looking for a better car. We make it through a long, tough week so we can enjoy a quiet weekend at home, and then the weekend arrives, and we start wishing that the weather was nicer. The gospel stories encourage us not to focus on what we lack but to notice all the things we have already and to take the time to appreciate them.

Jehoram was the only one healed that day who recognized and appreciated what had happened to him. He was with Dinah and Gemariah when the priest declared them clean. "Praise God!" he shouted with the priest. "Praise God!" Then he ran off to find Jesus, shouting and jumping as he went.

Jesus and his disciples were still making their way up the main road into town when Jehoram ran up to them. He fell at the feet of Jesus and thanked him again and again. "What happened to the rest of the group?" Jesus wondered aloud. Then he reached out his hand and helped Jehoram to his feet. "Go on your way," he instructed. "Your faith has saved you."

May we too take the time to notice what God has done for us and remember to be grateful.

Questions to ponder

- *What might be another reason that those cured of leprosy did not return to thank Jesus?*

- *For what gifts from God have you forgotten to say "thank you"?*

- *How do you cultivate a spirit of gratitude in your life?*

15
LIKE A RESOLUTE LOUISIANA HOMEOWNER
Mark 10:17–22

Eliab was a successful textile distributor with contacts throughout Judea and Samaria. He lived alone in a beautiful stone and cedar home outside of Jericho. Eliab attended Sabbath services at the synagogue as often as his travel schedule would allow and followed all the commandments. However, he wondered if there was any more to life than that. Hearing that the famous preacher from Galilee was visiting Jericho, Eliab rode into town, arriving just as Jesus was concluding his talk. He waited at a distance until Jesus had finished tending to the sick and the lame who crowded around.

Jesus, seated on a bench in front of a stand of cypress, noticed Eliab as he approached. Eliab abandoned his façade of self-confidence, because the teacher could see right through him. Eliab knelt in front of Jesus and asked his question, "Teacher, what must I do to have life?"

Jesus responded, "You know the commandments. Follow those."

Eliab persisted, "I have always followed the commandments. Is there anything else?"

Jesus felt affection for the man kneeling before him who had so many nice things but who was so dissatisfied with life. He looked intently at Eliab and extended an invitation. "Sell what you have, give the money to the poor, and follow me."

For a moment, Eliab caught a glimpse of the wonderful opportunity that was just within reach but could not bring himself to grab hold of it. Instead, he concluded that the invitation was foolishness. "I can't do that," he said softly. He stood up and walked away sad.

The rich man is a compelling character. I imagine that many of us feel sympathy for him. Eliab had a good heart and tried to do the right thing. He wanted to stay close to God and enjoy the life God had to offer. Jesus invited him to get rid of his possessions and join his company. We can certainly understand Eliab's reluctance. He had a nice home and a comfortable life. Leaving all that behind would be difficult. At the same time, we know that the rich man missed a golden opportunity. He had a chance to be a friend and a follower of Jesus. He had a chance to find life, a treasure in a field more precious than a hundred houses, and passed up the opportunity.

The rich man is like a wealthy resident of Louisiana in the path of a hurricane. She hunkers down in her beautiful home, having declined the invitation from her daughter and son-in-law to stay with them in Houston. Some emergency preparedness volunteers stop by the house to offer some help. The woman asks the volunteers what she must do to stay safe. They tell her that she needs to board up her windows and store clean water and supplies in the attic.

The woman tells them that she has done all that. Then they say that there is one more thing that she needs to do. If she wants to be sure to stay alive, she needs to leave her possessions behind and come with them. Regrettably, the woman in Louisiana declines the offer.

Part of what makes the gospel story compelling is that we never find out what happened to the rich man. We would like to believe that his life turned out okay, that he missed a great opportunity but continued to live a good life and managed to stay close to God. Perhaps his many possessions were not such a serious problem. The rich man may not have helped the poor as much as he might have, but God is merciful. We would like to think that the rich man made it to heaven after all.

We would like to think that things turned out fine for the woman in the path of the hurricane too. Maybe she lost power and the first floor of her home was flooded, but she made it through unharmed. We would like to think that the boarded-up windows and the supplies in the attic were enough to keep her safe. Then again, we are probably more realistic than that. We know that not everyone survives a hurricane and that it is foolish to take a chance. Emergency preparedness personnel know what they are talking about. They do not recommend evacuation unless things are really serious.

If that is the case, the rich man in the gospel story was foolish too. Perhaps Jesus really did know what he was talking about. Perhaps he recommended that the rich man sell his possessions because Jesus saw troubles ahead. The rich man should have listened to him. Of course, that raises questions for us. Is Jesus trying to tell us something and are we listening to him? Is Jesus asking us to get rid of some of our possessions? Is he inviting us to let go of something else? Perhaps Jesus extends the invitation because he recognizes troubles ahead.

A more realistic hope for Eliab is that he thought better of his decision later in life. The disciples continued to spread the gospel message after Jesus was gone. Perhaps Andrew, John, or Mary Magdalene made their way back to Jericho one day and Eliab decided to accept their invitation. We often assume that the rich man was young. We like to think that foolishness is the prerogative of youth and that Eliab made better decisions later in life.

That is a possibility for the woman in Louisiana too. Perhaps another rescue team would come by when the storm started pounding down and the woman would agree to leave. Perhaps there would be a dramatic helicopter rescue before the rushing waters washed her away. We might have a similar opportunity. We might be young and foolish now, not paying much attention to the advice Jesus gives. But invitations from Jesus are rarely a one-time-only offer. If Jesus does not get through to us this year, he will very likely try again next year. God never gives up on us.

Of course, we do not know what happened to Eliab. Perhaps he did not have as much time as we imagine. Maybe the rich man ran out of time. Even if he received another invitation sometime later in his life, there is no guarantee that his response would have been any different. As time went on, it probably became harder and harder for him to change. Maybe God tried every trick in the book to save him, but the rich man never accepted the life God had to offer. Maybe he was like a homeowner in Louisiana who remained resolute, a woman who decided to stay with her possessions no matter what and who eventually was washed away in the storm.

We are invited to consider that possibility in our own lives. There is no guarantee that we will even be around next year. Even if we are, we might become so set in our ways that change will be difficult. The story of the rich man invites us not to put things off too long. We are invited to listen to what Jesus might have to say to us today. He wants us to have life, real life, full of love, service, and hope. Maybe Jesus recognizes that there is something getting in the way of that, and he is inviting us to let go. We do not have to be strong, virtuous, or generous. We do not have to do it all on our own. Jesus will be with us and give us all the help we need. All we have to do is say yes.

Questions to ponder

- *In what ways would the rich man's life have improved if he had sold all his possessions and followed Jesus?*

- *What good gifts from God (material or otherwise) might you be holding a little too tightly?*

- *What was something you had to forsake when you made a major commitment in your life?*

PART 5

A final confrontation in Jerusalem

16
TOO MUCH HUBBUB!
John 2:13–16

The Temple in Jerusalem was buzzing with activity. Crowds of people from all over the Near East had come for the celebration of Passover. One group was swarming around the makeshift stalls to purchase pigeons and goats. Pigeons were terribly overpriced in the Temple, but travelers to Jerusalem generally did not bring their own pigeons with them. Several people were queued up at the currency exchange tables so that they could buy pigeons or pay the Temple tax with coins that were accepted in the Temple. Some hubbub was understandable. The problem was that the pigeons, goats, tax forms, and currency exchanges created such havoc that people were distracted from what was most important. In the midst of the noise and confusion, people were hard pressed to put themselves in God's presence and to offer a simple prayer. The chaos prevented people of faith from coming together to give thanks and praise to God.

Jesus walked into the Temple with his disciples and could see the problem immediately. He grabbed a leather cord that was lying near one of the stalls and started swinging it around and barking out commands to the sheep and goats to direct them outside. As two angry livestock merchants started heading in his direction, Jesus threw down the cord and strode over to the currency exchange area. He grabbed the corner of a table and flipped it in the air. Coins and ledger pages flew everywhere. He shouted at the stunned bankers, "Get this stuff out of here! This is not a market but a house of prayer!"

Some of those whose business operations had been disrupted began calling for the Temple guard. The disciples stepped in and assured them that Jesus had made his point and that there would be no further disturbances.

Jesus' animated exhortation did not go over so well with the religious authorities. In fact, after the Temple incident the leaders started putting together plans to have Jesus arrested. That did not concern Jesus. He was never hesitant to challenge customs or institutions that caused people to lose sight of their relationship with God and with one another. He challenged the customs of fasting and tithing and the rules about Sabbath rest, so it is not surprising that Jesus stirred up trouble in the Temple to help redirect people's attention.

Where would Jesus show up today to stir up a little trouble and challenge a custom or two? He might show up at the gift shop at St. Patrick's Cathedral in New York City, turning over card racks and display cases, saying that the hubbub was making it hard for people to pray. However, cathedral gift shops are generally not too chaotic. Jesus would probably be concerned about other activities that are far more distracting.

I can imagine Jesus at a municipal soccer park on a Sunday morning. He would place orange cones at all the entrances to the parking lot and redirect people who tried to get in. He would say, "The final rounds of the junior high soccer tournament are canceled. Prizes will be awarded to all particiipants. Now go back home. Spend some quiet time with your family and with God." Organized sports for kids can be great, but somewhere along the line soccer and softball leagues got out of hand. Parents are constantly shuttling kids to practices and games. Sports activities can claim an entire weekend. If ever there were people who needed Sabbath rest and time to renew their relationships with God and one another, it is modern-day, over-scheduled parents and children.

Jesus might show up at a downtown office building at 6:30 on a Thursday night and start shutting off the lights and directing the overworked workers to go home. He would tell the supervisors that the employees had worked long enough and that they needed to reconnect with their families and attend to their lives outside of the office. He would encourage the supervisors to hire a few more employees and lighten the load of the current staff.

Jesus could probably find a bit of hubbub in all of our lives that he would want to address. Some of us might have the television going constantly, with news programs, reality shows, or sporting events. Jesus would stop by, cut the power to the house, and say, "How about a little time out for quiet and conversation?" For good measure Jesus might take our cell phones and throw them into the nearest trash receptacle in hopes that we might make some connection with people we encounter face to face.

We can understand why Jesus' visit to the Temple got people upset. We would probably be upset too if he started stirring up things in our lives. Jesus was not opposed to people buying pigeons or exchanging currency. Similarly, he does not advocate the end of soccer tournaments, office jobs, or cell phones. However, Jesus is concerned when those things take on a life of their own and begin to distract us from the life God wants for us. Jesus is worried that those things might interfere with our relationships with family, friends, and colleagues and might prevent us from growing closer to God. That is why he upended a table or two in the Temple that day.

Questions to ponder

- *Why was overturning a money changer's table such an effective strategy for Jesus?*

- *Where would Jesus find a little too much hubbub in your life these days?*

- *How do you make space in your busy life for quiet and prayer?*

17

ONE BROTHER'S SURPRISING RESPONSE

Matthew 21:28–32

Jesus stood on a stone walkway under a portico along the perimeter wall of the Temple and invited people to gather around. He informed the group that he had a story about two brothers and wanted to hear their opinion on the matter. The brothers' names were Nabal and Parmenas.

Parmenas was a friendly, easy-going guy, always ready with a smile. The type of guy who would say, "If there is anything I can do for you, do not hesitate to ask."

So his father asked. He explained that the vineyard could use a little work. The ground was as hard as cement and the vines were growing out of control. He asked his son to spade the ground around the plants and trim back some of the vines. Parmenas happily agreed to do the work, promising that he would get right on it just as soon as he got back from an errand. Well, one errand turned into two. Then he got into a discussion with the cook, and a friend came to visit. Pretty soon the day was done, and Parmenas had not yet made an appearance out in the vineyard.

To Jesus' listeners and to us, that part of the story sounds pretty familiar. There is more than a little truth to it. All of us

probably know folks like Parmenas. In fact, most of us probably recognize a little bit of Parmenas in ourselves.

God might invite us to take a little time during the day for
some quiet reflection and prayer. It sounds like a great idea
and we fully intend to give it a try. But we never seem to get
around to it. There always seems to be 101 other things that
take up our time.

Maybe we intend to be a little more generous with our
money, to provide financial help to people in need on a more
regular basis. We have even saved the brochures from the
Red Cross and Oxfam International. We are just waiting
until we have our financial footing. But a satisfactory footing never seems to come along.

Or maybe God is inviting us to love a little more our
grumpy next-door neighbor, the manager at work, or our
self-assured sister-in-law. Maybe he is inviting us to let go
of the anger, the envy, or the harsh criticism that stands in
the way. At church on Sunday we resolve to do just that and
to be more loving, but by Monday morning our enthusiasm
fades.

Many of us probably see a bit of Parmenas in ourselves.
That part of the story sounds very familiar. The surprise is
Nabal, the other brother. For Jesus, that is the best part of
the story.

Nabal is very different from his father's other son. He has
wild hair, a sour disposition, and a tattoo of a snake crawling
down his arm. He prefers to be left alone and routinely burns
a foul-smelling incense.

His dad approaches and tells Nabal about the vineyard
and all the work that needs to be done. He asks him to help

with the project. Nabal mumbles something about being busy and turns his attention to the incense pot.

A little later that day, however, the dad looks out the window and sees Nabal working away, breaking up the ground with a shovel and trimming back some of the overgrown vines. Sweat is pouring down his forehead and his shaggy beard. He even exchanges a friendly word with a neighbor who passes by. Nabal is the last one we would expect to see in the vineyard, but there he is.

When Jesus finished the story, he asked the crowd which of the two brothers did what his father wanted him to do. "Nabal!" was the quick response.

"Nabal. Exactly!" Jesus replied. "Tax collectors and prostitutes are entering the Kingdom of God ahead of some of the rest of you. They

97

listened to the preaching of John and changed their lives because of it."

For Jesus, that is the best part of the story, because it is true. There are Nabals right in our midst, folks who, at one time, may have been very far from God but are working in the vineyard now.

An ex-con who used to be very violent suddenly changes his ways and lets God back into his life. He brings a little Bible to work so he can read some Scripture during his lunch break. On Sundays he volunteers as an usher at the Pentecostal church in his neighborhood. Jesus invites us to notice how this least likely candidate finds time to pray.

A woman who is a regular guest at the homeless shelter, and whose life has been filled with bad decisions, learns to make the best of her situation. She shows the new folks on the street where they can find a place to sleep for the night. After she picks up a sandwich at the soup kitchen, she brings half to her friend who lives under a bridge. The woman will never have her financial footing but is generous just the same.

A high school dropout, teenage mother works as a waitress and smokes like a fiend. She has some faults but knows how to love. She often shares a laugh with the cooks in the kitchen and stands by her friends through thick and thin. Somewhere along the line she decided that life is too short to be angry or critical, so she left those things behind. Jesus invites us to notice her too.

Jesus invites us to notice all the least likely candidates working away in the vineyard. Somehow, God has found a home in their hearts. God is working in their lives, and amazing things are happening.

The parable is a reminder that God's grace is working in ways we never expect and with people we might forget to notice. The parable is also an encouragement: God's grace is already working in our own lives, and God can do even more if we are willing.

God can help us to pray as faithfully as the ex-con who ushers at the Pentecostal church, to be as generous as the homeless woman with half a sandwich to share, and to love like the high school dropout working down at the IHOP. There might be a bit of Parmenas in all of us, but there is a bit of Nabal too.

Questions to ponder

- *Why did Parmenas lose interest in working in the vineyard?*

- *In what unexpected places have you found God's grace at work?*

- *What special assignment has God asked you to undertake in the past few months?*

18

ARE YOU IN HIS COMPANY?

Luke 22:54–62

The night air was cold as Peter waited in the courtyard outside the high priest's house, so he moved closer to the fire. He was recognized almost immediately by a servant girl. She asked him: "Are you in his company?"

She was speaking about Jesus, who had been arrested a short time earlier. The high priest, in consultation with the Sanhedrin, had decided that he needed to put a stop to Jesus' disruptive preaching, so he dispatched the Temple guard to take him into custody. Peter had followed at a distance, not wanting to be too closely associated with Jesus.

A week earlier, Peter would have enthusiastically acknowledged that he was a follower of Jesus, but the situation had changed very suddenly. Never had Jesus looked so powerless and so alone. His company was now that of criminals. "Are you in his company?" the servant girl had asked. Peter did not know how to answer.

All of us, at one time or another, are presented with the same question: "Are you in his company?" The question might not be put in quite that way; perhaps it is merely a question we ask ourselves. But the question is as important for us as it was for Peter that night. Sometimes the question is easy; we say "Yes!" with great enthusiasm. Sometimes the question is much more difficult. We do not risk arrest if we answer in the affirmative, but the implications of our answer are just as serious.

Clare is a junior in college. One day it becomes clear that the life of her friend, Megan, is slowly and quietly falling apart. Megan's fondness for alcohol has become an addiction. Megan puts on a good show. She seems as confident and witty as ever. She is a writer for the student newspaper and a diligent student but drinks heavily every night, does not eat much, and has a mounting pile of excuses to cover her mistakes. Megan's other friends are not much help; they all like drinking too much. Clare knows that if she were to say anything, wrath and ridicule would be the immediate response.

Followers of Jesus would take the risk. They know that real love sometimes means saying things that a friend does not want to hear. Clare always considered herself a follower of Jesus. Faced with the challenge of confronting Megan, she now sees following Jesus in a new light. Clare hears the question that has become difficult to answer: "Are you in his company?"

Alan has been married for twenty-three years and has a daughter in college and a son in high school. He meets a wonderful woman who is the new director of public relations for his firm. She is personable and energetic and interested in all sorts of things. Alan has developed a friendship with her; they enjoy each other's company.

For Alan the friendship is a welcome relief from his life at home. His relationship with his children is awkward at best. He feels very distant from his wife. She spends a good deal of time complaining, criticizing, or watching television. Alan reflects on the commitment he made twenty-three years ago. It feels much like a millstone tied around his neck.

Followers of Jesus value commitments, putting one's hands to the plow and not looking back. Commitments allow one to choose a path in life rather than being stuck at the crossroads forever. Commitments make possible wonderful things in the lives of those who make them and in the lives of others too. Alan always considered himself a follower of Jesus. Faced with the challenge of a twenty-three-year-old commitment, he now sees following Jesus in a new light. Alan hears the question that has become difficult to answer: "Are you in his company?"

Maria is a pediatrician in a five-partner practice downtown. One night a homeless man is killed by a hit-and-run driver just outside the wall of her gated neighborhood. The homeless man had been walking in the street because there are no sidewalks outside the complex.

Maria did not have anything to do with the accident, but it shook her up and made her think. She thought about her condominium complex, about who was allowed inside the gates and who was not. She thought about her medical practice, about the children who could receive care there and the children who could not. She could not help thinking that something was terribly wrong.

Followers of Jesus try to break down the barriers that exist between races, religions, and social classes. They welcome the outcast and try to serve the poor. Maria always considered herself a follower of Jesus. Recent events have made following Jesus appear in a new light. Maria hears the question that now seems to have special urgency: "Are you in his company?"

At one time or another, all of us are with Peter in the courtyard warming ourselves by the fire, faced with a difficult question. Perhaps, like Peter, we give the wrong answer. It is just too hard to say "Yes!" We do not have the strength or the patience or the courage to say "Yes!" So we say, "No, not me. You must have me confused with someone else. I used to hang out with him once but not anymore." Jesus does not say much. He is so far away we could not hear him if he did. But he turns and looks at us. There is love in eyes, as always, and disappointment too. That is where the scene ends for now. It is a sad place to stop, but we know it is not the end of the story. God's work is not quite done. There will be new opportunities for Peter and for all of us to answer that important question.

Questions to ponder

- *What good would it have done for Peter to acknowledge to the servant girl that he knew Jesus?*

- *Has anyone ever betrayed your friendship? If so, why do you think it happened?*

- *When in your life has being a follower of Jesus been difficult?*

19
THE DARKNESS FIGHTS BACK
John 18:19—19:16

After his arrest, Jesus was brought before the Sanhedrin to stand trial. The high priest asked him a few questions and quickly came to the conclusion that Jesus was not going to back down. The council decided to bring Jesus to the Roman procurator the following morning and charge him with insurrection.

We might wonder how the situation became so perilous for Jesus so quickly. A consideration of the gospels suggests that Jesus' life was heading in the direction of its ultimate conclusion for quite a while. The world is filled with darkness and always has been. Jesus was light in the midst of that darkness, and the darkness fought back.

Jesus cast out the darkness of evil spirits when he healed people possessed by them. As Jesus approached, even before he said anything, the evil spirits became angry and agitated. They started shouting in the presence of the light. They recognized the opposition they faced and knew that soon they would be powerless.

Jesus brought the light of compassion and concern to places where it was not always welcome. Jesus healed a blind man and a woman crippled for many years. Powerful people objected. They did not want responsibility for the poor and the sick. They excused themselves from that responsibility and came up with all sorts of great arguments for why such people were not their concern. Jesus' life and actions threw all of that into question, so powerful people fought back. They questioned Jesus' actions and his faith. They said he was an opponent and a sinner who violated purity regulations and the rules for Sabbath rest.

Sometimes the opposition to Jesus confronted him directly. More often the opposition met in secret and quietly planned his downfall. Even perfectly innocent actions created trouble. Jesus stirred up agitation and resistance when he shared food with those who were hungry and accepted a dinner invitation from Zacchaeus the tax collector. Rumors started circulating that Jesus was a glutton and a drunkard.

Jesus broke down barriers that others worked hard to keep in place. Jesus refused to claim any honors for himself, he laughed with little children (as if he were a child himself), and he talked with women whom others thought should have been quiet. He said outrageous things like "blessed are the poor" and "love your enemies." He forgave a woman caught in adultery, he visited with Samaritans, and he touched a man with leprosy. Jesus was a troublemaker; he threw everything into question. He would not play by the rules and that angered people.

Jesus never curried favor with powerful people, although he had opportunities. He did not temper his teaching to make it more palatable. He did not downplay his commitments and concerns when those around him had other priorities. When he dined at the home of Simon the Pharisee, Jesus was compassionate toward the sinful woman who cried at his feet even though he knew that it would irritate his host. Jesus did not try to appear more devout and honorable just to win Simon's approval.

Simon the Pharisee could have helped Jesus if he cooperated. Simon had some connections in Jerusalem; he could smooth things over. If Jesus wanted an open invitation to all the synagogues in the region, Simon could arrange it. Jesus just needed to be less insistent and learn to get along. But Jesus would not play that game.

If Simon had been with Jesus at the very beginning of his public life, in the desert for forty days, he would have realized that Jesus was not going to compromise. Satan made Jesus the very same offers of influence and honor, but Jesus refused. Jesus continued to refuse to the very end.

The chief priests brought Jesus to Pilate and charged him with insurrection, explaining that Jesus had claimed to be the King of the Jews. Pilate was a reasonable man. He did not care what Jesus believed. He just wanted Jesus to say that he was not a king and not a threat to Caesar and everything would be fine. Pilate wanted Jesus simply to play along. The Roman government did not want trouble. They did not want agitation; they just wanted people to be docile and compliant. That is why they were quick to arrest the insurrectionist Barabbas. The Romans would have killed him in a heartbeat. But suddenly and surprisingly the country preacher from Galilee turned out to be even more trouble. So they quickly killed him instead.

Questions to ponder

- *Why were religious leaders in Jesus' day so insistent on purity laws, and why did Jesus violate those laws so often?*

- *When have you had a firsthand experience of darkness or evil in the world?*

- *How might you help to break down a societal barrier?*

PART 6

Wondrous new life

20
BIG PLANS FOR THE KINGDOM OF GOD
Mark 16:1–8

In the 1860s, Denver was a small town in the middle of nowhere, known primarily for booze and gambling. John Evans, the governor, and Bill Byers, the newspaper editor, had higher hopes for Denver than that. They had visions of Denver becoming a major city, the capital of the Rocky Mountain west. Evans and Byers spent considerable energy trying to convince the Union Pacific Railroad that the best route from Omaha to San Francisco was straight through Denver. The railroad disagreed; the Colorado Rockies were too high and too treacherous. Wyoming would provide an easier route, so they built the line through Cheyenne. Of all the indignities!

A lot of go-getters moved to Cheyenne, leaving Denver in the dust. It looked like Denver would never amount to much. But Evans and Byers never gave up on the dream and convinced other Denverites to stick with them. The voters approved a bond issue to construct a railway line to Cheyenne. Lots of people donated labor to help get it built. In the summer of 1870 the line was complete, and Denver was connected to the rest of the country. Soon other railroads

began to build their lines to Denver, providing valuable connections to mining and ranching communities in Colorado and beyond. Industry and commerce began to expand in Denver along with the population. Denver was going to be a major player after all.

Centuries earlier, Jesus had even bigger plans than Evans and Byers. Much bigger plans. He wanted to build the Kingdom of God right here on earth. A kingdom of love and faith, of gratitude and generosity, of reconciliation and service. The Kingdom would be unlike any other kingdom on earth. It would not depend on wealth or military power. It would not be controlled by a few influential people. The Kingdom would depend on God's grace, and everyone was invited to take a part, those who were poor or outcasts of society, widows and Samaritans, righteous people and sinners. God would transform the world through them.

The followers of Jesus came to believe that such a Kingdom was possible and knew that they could never do it on their own. They knew that, without Jesus, the Kingdom of God was impossible. So when Jesus was arrested, prospects for the Kingdom looked bleak. When Jesus was killed, his followers were ready to give up hope. Then a surprising thing happened.

Early in the morning following the Sabbath, Mary Magdalene and two other women hiked to the cave in which Jesus had been buried after his execution. They brought spices to anoint the body. To their surprise, the stone that had covered the entrance to the tomb had been pushed aside. Mary quickly lit her oil lamp and led the group inside. A young man in a white robe sat quietly near the entrance, and the body of Jesus was missing. The women were dumbstruck.

"Jesus of Nazareth is not here," the young man said. "He has been raised from the dead."

An empty tomb and a message that Jesus had been raised. That was the only evidence the women had, but that was enough. They hurried off to tell the other disciples, leaving lamps and spices behind. The disciples began to have hope again.

Jesus, their teacher and their friend, was alive. God had not abandoned the world. By raising his Son, God revealed that Jesus' words were true. Light is more powerful than darkness, goodness is stronger than evil, and life is more powerful than death, for Jesus and all his followers. The Kingdom would continue to grow even in the face of obstacles and in the midst of apparent failure. Somehow, Jesus would continue to lead and guide it.

We are invited to share the same faith and the same hope as those first disciples. We do not have a nice young man in a white robe to explain to us what it all means. But we have Saints Mark, Matthew, Luke, and John to help us understand. We believe that God speaks through them. Jesus does not appear to us in quite the same way as he appeared to his first followers, but we experience Jesus in our own lives even so. And we trust the experiences of those who have preceded us. Through shared experiences of Jesus, our faith and hope are strengthened.

As it turns out, Denver did become a major city just like John Evans and Bill Byers had imagined. Denver eventually became a railway hub. And when automobiles hit the scene, interstate highways were built right through the center of town. Then Denver constructed an airport and then an even bigger one so it would be connected to the whole world. When interplanetary space travel takes off, Denver will likely be in the mix again, so that travelers to Jupiter do not need a stopover in Cheyenne.

But even if that does not happen. Even if Denver is not around in a thousand years, we believe that the Kingdom of God will be. God's plan for a Kingdom of love, justice, and peace will never fail. And Jesus will continue to lead and guide that Kingdom just like he promised.

Questions to ponder

- *If a city like Denver needs railroad lines and interstate highways to keep thriving, what does the Kingdom of God need?*

- *What positive change in the world over the last two thousand years might be evidence that the Kingdom of God has grown?*

- *When have you experienced hope during the past year?*

21
BARBECUED FISH BREAKFAST
John 21:1–14

A short time after I joined the Jesuits, I was sent with a fellow novice to the small town of Dangriga, Belize, to work in a parish there. The first few weeks were pretty tough. I really missed all the comforts of home and was slow to adjust to the new culture. More than that, I was not quite sure how I could be of help; it seemed like I was just getting in the way.

One afternoon, my novice companion and I were sitting around, hot and discouraged and covered with mosquito bites, when the assistant pastor, Father Frank, walked in. Frank was a tough, old-time missionary who worked hard, lived very simply, and ate mostly rice and beans. When he saw us sitting there, he said, "You know, I was thinking of baking a chocolate cake. How does that sound?"

We told him that it sounded pretty good. Frank was the last person I expected to bake a chocolate cake, but he did a great job. And later that day as we were enjoying the cake together, things did not seem quite so bad.

A few weeks after Jesus had appeared to the disciples in Jerusalem, a group of them were back in Galilee feeling a bit discouraged. Even though Jesus had risen from the dead, he was not with them in the same way as before, and they missed him. Moreover, the disciples did not know exactly what they were supposed to do next.

They had enjoyed some initial success in Jerusalem, but things were not going so well now. They wanted to reach out to the poor but did not know how; they hardly had any money themselves. They questioned the value of their preaching; people seemed to lose interest pretty quickly. Recently some Pharisees had been criticizing their instruction, and the disciples were not quite sure how to respond. The Kingdom of God was beginning to look to them like an impossible dream, something they could never manage on their own. So they went fishing.

Peter and Andrew got the family fishing boat ready; John and James borrowed nets from their father, Zebedee. For the four experienced fishermen, the expedition was like old times. Neither Bartholomew nor Thomas knew much about fishing but went along for the ride. By the time the disciples pushed the boat away from shore, the sun had already set.

They spent the entire night casting their nets but to no avail. They could not catch a thing. Peter began to wonder if he and his brother had lost whatever fishing talent they once had. At daybreak, a stranger called out from the shore, "Have you caught anything?"

"No," came the curt response.

"Try throwing the net over the right side of the boat," suggested the stranger.

With little enthusiasm, the disciples followed the instructions. To their amazement, they immediately began to feel an encouraging tug on the net. A few minutes later, when they pulled up the net, so many fish filled it that they could not lift it into the boat.

Suddenly, John realized who the stranger was. "It is the

Lord!" he shouted to Peter as he worked to secure his end of the net. Peter jumped into the water and swam for shore as the others began bringing the boat to shore, hauling the overloaded net along with them.

Jesus helped them catch a big boatload of fish that day and then fixed them a good breakfast. That breakfast on the shore of the Sea of Tiberias is one of the nicest stories in the whole gospel. Jesus knew that the disciples were discouraged and uncertain, so he wanted to spend a little more time with them before he ascended into heaven. He wanted to plan something that would lift their spirits. Jesus knew that the disciples liked to eat, so he brought some bread and got a fire started and began barbecuing the fish.

The disciples enjoyed the meal immensely. They were famished, the bread was fresh, and the fish was cooked just right. Jesus always had a knack for grilling fish. As they enjoyed the food, they also enjoyed the setting. The sea was particularly beautiful that morning.

Most of all, the disciples enjoyed being with Jesus. It was just like old times. They shared stories, laughed, and dreamed about what might come next. Simply being with Jesus got the disciples back on track. Once again, they could see the world through his eyes; their hope for the Kingdom of God was restored. They did not get all the plans for the future worked out, but that was okay. Jesus would be with them through it all; he would give them all the help they needed.

The breakfast on the shore contains a message for us too, a message about kindness and hope. Jesus cares for us, just as he cared for those early disciples. He recognizes those times when we are uncertain or discouraged, and he wants to do something nice for us. He would fix us breakfast if he could. Usually, he finds other ways to reach out to us, by working in the lives of good people who believe in him. Their kindness to us is a sign of his kindness too. Jesus cannot bake us a chocolate cake but can inspire a tough, old follower of his to do it for him. And he can inspire us to return the favor. We are all in this together and a little kindness goes a long way. Jesus invites us to keep an eye out for an opportunity to do something nice for someone who might need it.

The breakfast story is also a story about hope. Sometimes the Kingdom of God seems like an impossible dream to us; we are not sure what we are supposed to do next. Jesus encourages us not to give up hope. The Kingdom of God never comes off without a hitch. It is always two steps forward and one step back. All of us will encounter failure, uncertainty, and disappointment from time to time, but Jesus is right there with us even though we do not always realize it. He can lead and inspire us, point us in the right direction, and give us confidence even in the face of long odds. Jesus can transform our simple efforts. All we have to do is throw the net into the water; Jesus will make sure that it gets filled with fish.

Questions to ponder

- *Why was sharing meals with friends and followers so important to Jesus?*

- *What is your primary vocation or life's work and why does Jesus consider it valuable?*

- *When has someone provided needed encouragement to you during challenging times?*

SELECT BIBLIOGRAPHY

Brown, Raymond E., SS, and Raymond F. Collins. "Canonicity." Brown et al. 1034–54.

Brown, Raymond E., SS, Joseph A. Fitzmyer, SJ, and Roland E. Murphy, OCarm, ed. *The New Jerome Biblical Commentary*. Englewood Cliffs: Prentice Hall, 1990.

Buechner, Frederick. *Peculiar Treasures: A Biblical Who's Who*. San Francisco: HarperCollins Publishers, 1979.

— . *Telling the Truth: The Gospel as Tragedy, Comedy, and Fairy Tale*. San Francisco: Harper & Row, 1977.

Campbell, Anthony F., SJ, and James W. Flanagan. "1–2 Samuel." Brown et al. 145–59.

Clifford, Richard J., SJ, and Roland E. Murphy, OCarm. "Genesis." Brown et al. 8–43.

Collins, Raymond F. "Inspiration." Brown et al. 1023–33.

Donahue, John R., SJ, and Daniel J. Harrington. *The Gospel of Mark*. Sacra Pagina Series, Volume 2. Collegeville: Liturgical Press, 2002.

Gench, Frances Taylor. *Back to the Well: Women's Encounters with Jesus in the Gospels*. Louisville: Westminster John Knox Press, 2004.

Harrington, Daniel J., SJ. "The Gospel According to Mark." Brown et al. 596–629.

— . *The Gospel of Matthew*. Sacra Pagina Series, Volume 1. Collegeville: Liturgical Press, 2007.

Johnson, Luke Timothy. *The Gospel of Luke*. Sacra Pagina Series, Volume 3. Collegeville: Liturgical Press, 1991.

Karris, Robert J., OFM. "The Gospel According to Luke." Brown et al. 675–721.

King, Philip J., and Lawrence E. Stager. *Life in Biblical Israel*. Louisville: John Knox Press, 2001.

Martin, James, SJ. *Jesus: A Pilgrimage*. New York: HarperCollins Publishers, 2014.

Meier, John P. "Jesus." Brown et al. 1316–28.

Moloney, Francis J., SDB. *The Gospel of John*. Sacra Pagina Series, Volume 4. Collegeville: Liturgical Press, 1998.

Perkins, Pheme. "The Gospel According to John." Brown et al. 942–85.

Puhl, Louis J., SJ. *The Spiritual Exercises of St. Ignatius, Based on Studies in the Language of the Autograph*. Chicago: Loyola, 1951.

Stuhlmueller, Carroll, CP. "Deutero-Isaiah and Trito-Isaiah." Brown et al. 329–48.

Tylenda, Joseph N., SJ. *A Pilgrim's Journey: The Autobiography of Ignatius of Loyola*. Wilmington: Michael Glazier, 1985.

Viviano, Benedict T., OP. "The Gospel According to Matthew." Brown et al. 630–74.

Wright, Addison G., SS, Roland E. Murphy, OCarm, and Joseph A. Fitzmyer, SJ. "A History of Israel." Brown et al. 1219–52.